Literature Review

THE PRINCIPAL-AGENT PROBLEM IN FINANCE

Sunit N. Shah

CFA Institute Research Foundation

Statement of Purpose

The CFA Institute Research Foundation is a not-for-profit organization established to promote the development and dissemination of relevant research for investment practitioners worldwide.

ISBN 978-1-934667-72-9

April 2014

Editorial Staff

Ellen Barber
Editor

Cindy Maisannes
Manager, Publications Production

Randy Carila
Publishing Technology Specialist

The Principal–Agent Problem in Finance

Sunit N. Shah
Strategist
Pine River Capital Management

The relationship between a principal and the agent who acts on the principal's behalf contains the potential for conflicts of interest. The principal–agent problem arises when this relationship involves both misaligned incentives and information asymmetry. In asset management, factors contributing to the principal–agent problem include managers' compensation structures and investors' tendency to focus on short-term performance. In the banking industry, myriad principal–agent relationships and complex instruments provide a fertile breeding ground for incentive conflicts, many of which were highlighted by the recent financial crisis.

Introduction

Within economics, the study of incentives is a relatively new one. In fact, Joseph Schumpeter's (1954) thousand-plus-page authoritative survey, *History of Economic Analysis*, contains not a single mention of the word "incentive" (Laffont and Martimort 2002). The study of principal–agent relationships, an even newer phenomenon, resides within this framework. The principal is one who delegates a task to the agent, who performs the task on the principal's behalf. Everyday examples of this relationship include a homeowner using a real estate agent to sell a house and a business owner hiring a manager to run a store. Within this construct, whenever the two entities' interests are misaligned and monitoring is difficult, the agent could act in a way that does not reflect the principal's best interests. Such is the basis of the principal–agent problem.

Any system that includes such relationships is vulnerable to potential principal–agent problems; the financial system is no exception. Individuals in a variety of roles within this system, including investment managers, broker/dealers, rating agencies, and even the government, serve as agents in one form or another. Within asset management, compensation structures in large part drive managers' interests, and if these contracts are not structured correctly, managers may have an incentive to act counter to the fiduciary duty they have to their investors. Furthermore, investors' tendency to focus on short-term performance may indirectly provide managers with additional incentives that exacerbate this problem. Similar incentive problems exist within the banking industry, many of which were clearly illuminated by the 2008 financial crisis.

This literature review addresses these concerns to provide a better understanding of principal–agent relationships, and the associated potential problems, in finance.

Evolution of the Principal–Agent Problem. Initially, most economists concerned themselves principally with the mechanics of markets; guided by Adam Smith's "invisible hand," these markets generally function without a hitch (Laffont and Martimort 2002). As economics matured as a science, this analysis grew ever more granular over time. As Ronald Coase notes in his seminal paper "The Nature of the Firm" (1937), in the 1930s, the new trend among economists was toward beginning their analysis at the firm level rather than at the industry level. His work was a catalyst for much of the progress in this transition. Coase explores the question of why firms exist in the first place, as opposed to having every individual in an economy simply contract separately with every other. He concludes that it is rational for firms to exist when the costs of executing transactions on the open market exceed those of organizing the same transactions in a group setting (Coase 1937). Coase addresses individual worker incentives, monitoring, and the use of "authority" within an organization. The work of Coase and his contemporaries, however, maintained a high-level view of the firm and did not delve deeply into the incentives of individual workers or the conflicts those incentives might create.

As economic thought continued to progress, analysis shifted from firm-level behavior to intra-firm mechanics. Initially, models assumed that the individual members of a firm had identical utility functions, so all members of a given team had no motivation other than to work in tandem. It was not until the late 1950s and early 1960s that attention began to focus on the diversity of incentives across members of a given team, the inability to fully monitor all employees' behavior, and the problems that this combination causes for delegation (Laffont and Martimort 2002).

The study of these conditions initiated the subdiscipline of economics known as "optimal contract theory," which examines the conflict that can occur as a result of the delegation of tasks to an agent in the presence of incomplete information. Contract theory addresses two distinct sets of questions: those that arise before a contract is struck, including optimal methods of behavior, such as signaling and screening; and those that arise post-agreement, including actions caused by misaligned incentives, such as shirking behavior.

Meanwhile, in the 1960s and 1970s, another set of economists, including Kenneth Arrow and Robert Wilson, explored risk sharing among groups of people with different attitudes toward risk (Eisenhardt 1989). Wilson (1968), for example, examines what happens when a syndicated group of individuals needs to make a joint decision with an uncertain outcome, such as the debt/equity split for investing a joint $1 of capital in an uncertain venture. Spence and Zeckhauser (1971) tackle a slightly different problem; they explore several mathematical models of insurance contracts in which the insurer and the insured have different utility functions, the insurer has various monitoring abilities, and the insured has several choices of behavior available. Such analyses bring to light a set of difficulties that can occur when parties to a contract involving the exchange of risk alter their actions after the contract has been struck.[1] This area of investigation came to be known as "agency theory."

These two lines of study share a common thread: Both examine how one party to a contract must be wise to the possibility that the other party might change his or her behavior post-agreement. Consequently, these two paths merged over time. In this way, agency theory came to include the examination of post-contract behavior both in a cooperative framework with conflicting incentives and in the context of risk sharing among groups (Eisenhardt 1989). This combination came to represent the latter half of contract theory mentioned above and was eventually dubbed the "principal–agent model." The difficulty involved in structuring the optimal contract in the principal–agent model when the principal has to worry that the agent might act in a way that does not reflect the principal's interests has come to be known as the "principal–agent problem."

In their examination of insurance contracts, Spence and Zeckhauser (1971) find that, even with conflicting incentives, cases in which the insurer can monitor the insured's actions yield no issues because the insurer can simply structure the contract to yield the appropriate payoffs for each action the insured might take. Cases of incomplete monitoring, however, do create a problem:

> [When] a signal . . . depends in part or completely on the insured individual's action . . . [t]he insured will be induced to alter his natural maximizing action somewhat in order to influence this signal and thus increase his payoff from the insurer. The insurer can be cognizant of this adverse incentives problem, but he cannot overcome it. Given his limited information-monitoring capability, his selection of the optimal insurance payoff function is a second-best exercise. Neither complete risk spreading nor appropriate incentives for individual action will be achieved. To find the optimal mixture of these two competing objectives is a difficult problem, here as in the real world. (p. 387)

This outcome highlights a key component of agency research. For the principal–agent problem to be meaningful, two ingredients are needed: conflicting incentives and private information. Without the former, the principal may simply leave the agent to his or her own devices; without the latter, the principal need only structure the contract to cover each realization of the private information *ex post*. Consequently, for a principal–agent relationship to

[1]See Arrow (1971) for a thorough treatment of this topic.

exhibit the principal–agent problem, both characteristics must exist (Laffont and Martimort 2002).

Although the above conclusion arose through an examination of risk sharing within a group, it applies to agency research in general, including contracting within a firm. Consider a store owner who aims to hire a manager to run her store. On the one hand, if the owner and manager have the same incentives—say, if the manager is the owner's husband—then the owner may simply engage the manager without fear that he might act in a way counter to her interests. On the other hand, if the owner can perfectly monitor the manager's effort—say, through security cameras or network logs—she can simply structure the contract to contain a large penalty in any situation involving a lack of effort on the manager's part. Only if the manager has both different incentives from the owner and the ability to shirk his responsibilities undetected might principal–agent problems arise.

Several works in the 1970s brought the study of the principal–agent relationship into sharper focus. Ross (1973) examines classes of utility functions and payoff structures in which the solution to the principal's problem leads to Pareto efficiency, or outcomes in which no one party can be made better off without making another party worse off. Jensen and Meckling (1976) explore agency costs to both the principal and the agent and examine the impact of such costs on a number of other variables, including the ownership structure of the firm, the fair market value of the firm's stock, and the firm's use of debt and equity. Harris and Raviv (1979) demonstrate the added value of monitoring in principal–agent relationships and explore the benefits of imperfect, or noisy, monitoring to the outcome of such arrangements. The study of principal–agent relationships has endured to this day, with several recent works addressing similar issues. As one example among many, Miller (2008) examines potential solutions to the principal–agent problem for various management patterns within a firm and concludes that there is no single solution to such problems. Instead, he constructs a contingency theory in which various conditions within the firm call for different solutions to any principal–agent problems that appear.[2]

Principal–agent problems arise naturally in a variety of economic relationships and contexts. Mas-Colell, Whinston, and Green (1995) provide the following list of examples in their exposition:

> [•] insurance companies and insured individuals (the insurance company cannot observe how much care is exercised by the insured),
>
> [•] manufacturers and their distributors (the manufacturer may not be able to observe the market conditions faced by the distributor),

[2]For a thorough review of the agency literature, see Eisenhardt (1989). For more detail on the principal–agent problem, see Mas-Colell, Whinston, and Green (1995) or Laffont and Martimort (2002).

[•] a firm and its workforce (the firm may have more information than its workers about the true state of demand for its products and therefore about the value of the workers' product), and

[•] banks and borrowers (the bank may have difficulty observing whether the borrower uses the loaned funds for the purpose for which the loan was granted). (p. 478)

The principal–agent problem itself contains two subcategories of conflict based on the informational asymmetry involved. The first, known as *adverse selection*, involves problems arising from hidden knowledge. The second, known as *moral hazard*, involves problems arising from hidden action. For example, an owner's incomplete knowledge of the abilities of a manager she considers hiring could cause an adverse selection problem, whereas the inability of that same owner to observe how hard the manager works once hired could produce a moral hazard problem (Mas-Colell et al. 1995).[3]

The Principal–Agent Problem in Finance. Any industry in which some individuals act on behalf of others faces potential principal–agent problems, and the finance industry is no exception. On the contrary, that the study of the principal–agent problem evolved as a merger of firm mechanics with the exploration of risk sharing among groups demonstrates how susceptible the financial system is to the consequences of this problem. Not only do financial markets include a number of intertwined relationships in which complete or perfect monitoring is difficult, but they also involve numerous transactions in which risk shifts from one party to another through insurance or insurance-like products. Therefore, those involved in financial markets must be that much more wary of the potential problems inherent in agency relationships. The extraordinary level of interconnectedness present in financial markets creates a fertile breeding ground for potential conflicts. Consider the path of a mortgage through the financial system:

- The bank that makes the loan must attempt to ensure that the individual borrowing the funds puts forth his or her best effort to guard against default.
- The packager that bundles this mortgage with others must ensure that it receives all of the pertinent information it needs from its counterparties and so must each of the relevant parties as the resulting mortgage-backed securities (MBS) are packaged, repackaged, tranched, and sold downstream.

[3]Laffont and Martimort (2002) include a third category, *non-verifiability*, which exists when the principal and the agent have the same knowledge *ex post* but this knowledge cannot be verified by a third party, as in the case of a benevolent court of law attempting to make a ruling in a case between the two. This category receives notably less coverage in the literature than either of the two mentioned in the main text here.

- The buyers of the various resulting securities must also ensure that they receive all relevant information as insurance in the form of credit default swaps (CDS) is written against the resulting payments, as those CDS are packaged into collateralized debt obligations (CDOs), and as those CDOs are squared, cubed, and so on.
- The investment bank that packages the loans must ensure that its long-term interests and those of its employees executing the transactions are aligned.
- The investor whose funds are used to purchase all or part of the resulting securities must ensure that the asset manager who executes those purchases does so to benefit the investment goals of the investor rather than the manager's own personal fee stream.
- The taxpayer must ensure, when there is an implicit guarantee by the government if a given firm fails, that that institution does not accumulate excess risk as a result of participating in upside outcomes with taxpayer insurance in the extreme downside.

Given the misaligned incentives involved and the difficulty of monitoring one's counterparty, ethical standards must be high to ensure that these actors' monetary incentives do not override their fiduciary ones.

In June 2013, a former assistant director and counsel in the US SEC enforcement division, then a partner at Labaton Sucharow, asked his law firm to conduct a survey on Wall Street ethics. The firm surveyed 250 insiders in the financial services industry, including traders, portfolio managers, investment bankers, hedge fund professionals, financial analysts, and stock brokers.

The survey found a number of unsettling results: 23% of respondents said they had observed wrongdoing in the workplace (Sorkin 2013), and 24% felt some of their colleagues likely had engaged in misconduct to get ahead (Labaton Sucharow 2013). These actors' incentive structures were cited as contributors to these outcomes: 26% of survey participants "believed the compensation plans or bonus structures in place at their companies incentivize employees to compromise ethical standards or violate the law" (Sorkin 2013, p. B1).

Furthermore, 17% stated that they believed company leaders would turn a blind eye if they suspected a top earner was engaged in insider trading, and 15% doubted that leadership would report such crimes even if they knew of them. It is not surprising, then, that 24% said they would "engage in insider trading to make $10 million if they could get away with it" (Sorkin 2013, p. B1). The fact that many of these results were disproportionately skewed toward the younger members of these organizations paints a pretty grim picture of the future of leadership in the industry. In the survey administrator's own words:

> A particularly troubling and consistent finding from our survey is what the future holds for Wall Street. Many of the young professionals who will one day assume control of the trillions of dollars that the industry manages have lost their moral compass, accepted corporate wrongdoing as a necessary evil and fear reporting misconduct. This is a ticking economic time bomb that responsible organizations must immediately defuse. (Labaton Sucharow 2013, p. 1)

Many of the respondents work at firms whose codes of ethics specifically proscribe those behaviors. JPMorgan Chase's code states, "Our integrity and reputation depend on our ability to do the right thing, even when it's not the easy thing"; Goldman Sachs's code states, "No financial incentive or opportunity—regardless of the bottom line—justifies a departure from our values" (Sorkin 2013, p. B1). Wrongdoing in the financial services industry also runs counter to the CFA Institute Code of Ethics and Standards of Professional Conduct, which states, among other things, that members and candidates must do the following:

> • Place the integrity of the investment profession and the interests of clients above their own personal interests. . . .
>
> • Practice and encourage others to practice in a professional and ethical manner that will reflect credit on themselves and the profession.
>
> • Promote the integrity of and uphold the rules governing capital markets.[4] (p. 1)

Other surveys have yielded similar results. CFA Institute, in conjunction with Edelman, conducted its own survey on trust in the industry. The study found that only 53% of investors trust investment management firms to do what is right. This figure varies by geographical region, dipping as low as 39% in the United Kingdom. Similar figures hold for the financial services industry, with only 52% of investors, including only 33% of those in the United Kingdom, trusting its members (CFA Institute and Edelman 2013).

These results emerge despite the importance of trust to investors. In the same survey, the attribute investors cited most often as the most important when making an investment manager hiring decision was "Trusted to act in my best interest," a response given more than twice as often as "Ability to achieve high returns." The top three attributes that investors identified as building that trust—"Has transparent and open business practices," "Takes responsible actions to address an issue or crisis," and "Has ethical business practices"—all relate to integrity rather than performance (CFA Institute and Edelman 2013). They also directly reflect the problems inherent in the principal–agent model: Investors want a greater ability to view and monitor

[4]CFA Institute, "Code of Ethics and Standards of Professional Conduct" (1 July 2010): http://www.cfapubs.org/toc/ccb/2010/2010/14.

their agents' behavior, and they want to trust their agents to act responsibly in scenarios in which they themselves cannot participate.

In truth, the majority of actors in this space are not to be vilified. As Sorkin (2013) states, "There are clearly good people out there doing good work. A large majority fall in that category" (p. B1). But when 28% of industry insiders think "the financial services industry does not put the interests of clients first" (Sorkin 2013, p. B1), that is 28% too many.

Roadmap. This literature review explores the academic research behind the principal–agent problem in the finance industry today. The discussion focuses on two categories within the financial system: (1) asset management and (2) banking and related activities. It begins with an analysis of compensation structures in asset management. The structure of asset management contracts directly drives the incentives that govern how managers will invest their clients' money; if these incentives are not aligned with those of the investors, principal–agent problems may ensue. The discussion then moves to the tendency of investors to focus on short-term performance, known as investor "short-termism." This tendency on the part of investors creates short-term incentives for managers and, consequently, may indirectly cause managers to act in ways that do not reflect the long-term interests of those very investors.

The narrative then shifts to the banking industry, using the financial crisis of 2008 as a backdrop. The banking industry contains many potential principal–agent problems, including some entirely of its own, and the recent experience provided by the crisis illuminates many of these issues within a real-life framework. This section takes a detailed look at this important event from recent history to demonstrate examples of these issues. It expands the discussion on compensation structures to other entities, such as bank management, traders, and rating agencies. It also examines the role of the government in both the crisis and its aftermath, as well as the principal–agent issues that may have arisen as a result.

Compensation Structures in Asset Management

Although many nonpecuniary factors are often involved in an asset management contract, the compensation structure itself commonly represents the main determinant of the manager's incentives. Investment managers have a fiduciary responsibility to act in their investors' best interests, regardless of their own. But investors who trust their funds with asset managers generally cannot perfectly monitor the level of effort the managers put forth, and asset-level detail on where their funds are placed is often either unavailable or costly to acquire. Consequently, if an investor's incentives are not aligned with those of the manager, the manager often has both an incentive to act counter to the investor's best interests and the ability to do so undetected. Given the magnitude of payment generally involved in asset management contracts, misaligned incentives have significant potential to override a manager's fiduciary responsibility to his or her clients. Structuring such contracts optimally is, therefore, of the utmost importance.

Traditional Contract Structures. As a category, asset management contains a diverse set of investment strategies. Despite the major differences across these investment categories, compensation terms are often similar. Generally, investment managers receive two streams of fee revenue. The first, called a "management fee," is typically a percentage of the assets under management (AUM) and is often justified by overhead expenses, such as rent, technology infrastructure, and the fixed portion of payroll. The second stream of revenue generally represents a percentage of the return created by the manager net of the management fee. This fee stream is commonly termed the "performance fee" or "incentive fee" and is often applied only to the return generated above the portfolio's previous maximum value, called the "high-water mark."[5]

■ *Management fee vs. incentive fee.* Because the management fee represents a payment equal to a specific percentage of the fund's assets, both the management fee and the investors' assets grow based on the return to the fund. Consequently, along this dimension, the manager's incentives and those of the investors are aligned. The management fee can be viewed as essentially a small equity stake for the manager in the fund. Investors often ask managers to coinvest with them in their funds as a way of amplifying this effect without paying larger management fees.

The performance fee, in contrast, gives the manager a strong incentive on the upside to provide additional effort at the margin to increase the fund's return. According to Goetzmann, Ingersoll, and Ross (2003), among others, the incentive fee can be treated like a call option in the sense that the manager participates in any upside above the high-water mark but does not suffer from any downside below it. Essentially, the performance fee gives the manager the option to purchase an equivalent percentage of the fund at that same percentage of the high-water mark. That is, if a manager receives a 20% performance fee, he or she has a fee stream equivalent to the option to purchase 20% of the fund at 20% of the high-water mark.

In one sense, then, the trade-off between the management fee and the incentive fee boils down to a question of equity compensation versus option compensation. Management fees provide the manager with a moderate level of direct alignment with the investor's interests in all scenarios, whereas

[5]Although different areas within asset management generally structure compensation contracts similarly, some often use different terminology. For simplicity, the discussion here will stick with the terms "management fee" and "incentive fee."

incentive fees provide a larger incentive on the upside to produce alpha but also potentially provide an incentive to introduce more volatility and make riskier investments. The optimal contract balances the trade-off between the motivations in the equity-like compensation of the management fee and those in the option-like compensation of the incentive fee.

- *Optimal contract structure—static framework.* Several papers on optimal compensation structure model these contracts in a static, one-period framework. Lambert and Larcker (2004) examine the incentive provided to an agent serving as management. Holding the cost of the contract to the principal constant, they compare the incentives provided by stock option plans of various strike prices with those provided by compensation in restricted stock. They find that restricted stock provides the least cost-effective method for properly incentivizing the agent from the principal's point of view. Restricted stock incentivizes the agent better when incentives are low, such as when the stock price has dropped significantly below its starting value, whereas stock options incentivize the agent better when incentives are high, such as when the options are close to being at the money.

Agarwal, Daniel, and Naik (2009) examine the same question in a fund management context by extending the analysis of Goetzmann et al. (2003) one step further. They recognize that the various investors in a fund enter that fund at different times and with different initial investments. Consequently, they consider the manager's overall pay as a portfolio of call options, with each call option on a portion of a given investor's wealth in the fund struck at the high-water mark that prevailed when that particular investor invested. The manager's incentives are then driven by the increase in the value of the portfolio of options given each relevant high-water mark and the relative size of each investment.

Agarwal et al. (2009) calculate, for each option in the portfolio, its "delta," or the increase in that option's value for a one percentage point increase in the value of the underlying fund. Then, they calculate the delta for all of the options across the portfolio. Combining this portfolio delta with the manager's incentive based on his or her coinvestment in the fund yields the manager's overall incentive to increase the value of the fund by another dollar, which they term the manager's "total delta." This analysis is similar to the analysis of executive compensation in other management contexts, which often uses deltas from the portfolio of stocks and options held by CEOs to estimate their incentives to drive value increases in their firms (Agarwal et al. 2009).

The authors find that the performance fee percentages themselves serve as a poor representation of the manager's incentive to increase the value of the fund. Funds with the same incentive fee structure exhibit notably different total deltas as a consequence of differences in the return histories of individual capital flows. Within their data, they find the correlation between total delta and the incentive fee to be only 0.17. Furthermore, they find that total delta does explain future returns, even after incentive fees are controlled for, whereas incentive fees do not explain future returns after total delta is controlled for (Agarwal et al. 2009).

They also find that high-water marks and hurdle rates are positively related to future returns, lending support to the use of these elements as a method to align the managers' incentives with those of the investors. Elements that might suggest more managerial discretion, such as longer lockup, notice, and redemption periods, are also positively related to investment returns. It is not immediately clear, however, whether any of these correlations are causal in nature. The authors also find that the manager's coinvestment in a fund relates positively to performance, which suggests further that the management fee may be a valuable tool in aligning the incentives of the manager with those of the investors (Agarwal et al. 2009).

- *Optimal contract structure—dynamic framework.* Lan, Wang, and Yang (2013) examine a similar question in a different, purely theoretical, context. They seek to determine the optimal amount of leverage a manager can employ as a function of the parameters of the contract and the fund's current position relative to its high-water mark (HWM). They use the option framework from Goetzmann et al. (2003) and Agarwal et al. (2009) but in a dynamic model in which the manager seeks to maximize the discounted present value of his or her fees over time. Within this setting, Lan et al. calculate the optimal amount of leverage both from the manager's point of view and from that of the investors.

They examine the effect of the contract structure on the manager's desired leverage and compare this amount of leverage with what is optimal for the investors. As the incentive fee increases, holding the total cost of the contract constant, the equity-like position of the management fee gets replaced with a call-option-like position in the fund's assets, which changes the manager's incentives. When the AUM is very far from the HWM, the manager has a relatively low incentive to increase the AUM an additional percentage point because the increase in the value of the manager's option would be small. As the AUM approaches the HWM, the delta of the manager's position increases. This effect increases his or her incentive to grow the AUM an additional percentage point, providing motivation to increase the leverage employed in the fund's strategy. Lan et al. find that the management fee perfectly aligns the managers' incentives with those of the investors. When there is no incentive fee, the manager employs the amount of leverage that is also optimal for investors as a result of the equity-like characteristics of the management fee structure (Lan et al. 2013).

The authors then take the analysis one step further, incorporating a liquidation option in the case of a large drawdown, representing a loss of investor confidence in the manager's abilities and a resulting desire on the part of the investors to cut their losses. This extension reflects the idea that a large enough loss might trigger significant redemptions, resulting in a closing of the fund and, therefore, a loss of all future management and incentive fee streams. From the manager's point of view, the liquidation is exogenously imposed once the AUM reaches a predetermined percentage of the high-water mark. This feature of the model essentially imposes a short put position on the manager in addition to the long call position provided by the incentive fee. With this liquidation option included, the authors rerun the analysis and examine the results (Lan et al. 2013).

They find that as the AUM approaches the liquidation point, the dynamics of this short put position cause the manager to reduce leverage rapidly, often going so far as to employ a leverage ratio less than 1—or, in other words, to invest part of the portfolio in the risk-free asset. This behavior, of course, defeats the investors' purpose in investing with the manager in the first place; they have placed money with the manager to take advantage of the alpha that manager generates, not to pay fees on a strategy that they could employ themselves (Lan et al. 2013).

The results imply that in a framework in which the manager and the investors have similar preferences for risk and the manager does not face a significant risk of redemptions, a pure management fee structure is optimal. The authors conclude, however, that the implications of the liquidation option cast doubt on the prevailing wisdom that high-powered incentive fees encourage excessive risk taking. They find that when facing the risk of redemptions, managers may invest more conservatively than is optimal for the investors. They state that this tendency could explain why investors often require a lower bound on a fund's leverage; otherwise, the manager might choose too conservative a path in order to ensure survival and fee collection in subsequent periods (Lan et al. 2013).

Lim, Sensoy, and Weisbach (2013) provide empirical support for this conclusion. They quantify the effect of increased performance on the future stream of capital flows—and, consequently, the future stream of management and performance fees—that a manager will receive. They find that for each dollar in value a manager creates, 83 cents goes to the investors and 17 cents goes to the manager, on average. The manager, however, receives an additional 58 cents in expected future management and incentive fees, yielding a total of 75 cents in additional income per dollar of value created. In other words, almost 80% of the income generated from an additional dollar of investment value comes in the form of fees on future capital flows. The authors find further that this number is notably higher for nascent funds; brand-new funds receive 84 cents in future income from each dollar of value created (Lim et al. 2013).

They also find that the effect of value creation from increasing capital inflows decreases monotonically and significantly over the life of a fund, with most of the additional capital entering in the first two years. Specifically, they find that a 10 percentage point increase in return corresponds to a 22% increase in AUM over the next two years for an existing fund and to a 41% increase in AUM over the next two years for a new fund. The diminishing effect is so strong that a steady decrease can be seen even at the quarterly level. They also find that funds that execute strategies they identify as capacity constrained receive a lower future capital incentive than those they deem unconstrained, along the lines of 64 cents versus 50 cents. This finding suggests that investors understand that some strategies can scale well whereas others will have trouble generating the same alpha at higher levels of assets under management.

Lim et al. (2013) also find, curiously, that the direct and indirect incentives of the agent are positively correlated in their sample. In other words, firms that charge higher fees and, therefore, receive higher current compensation for a dollar increase in value creation also receive higher future compensation from the same dollar of value created. This result contradicts optimal contracting theory, under which equilibrium is reached only when the total incentive to each agent in the market remains constant across agents. This finding likely reflects the fact that some characteristics of a fund, such as having a well-known management team or an in-vogue strategy, allow the fund to both charge higher fees and create more buzz if the fund outperforms others. This explanation could also lend credence to the existence of the "illusion of validity," or the tendency for individuals to place too much weight on new evidence that supports a previously held conclusion (Burton and Shah 2013). Investors might react even more strongly to above-average returns in funds they already believe have top-flight management, as is likely the case if the fund has above-average fees and they are already invested in it.

These results imply that if managers are at all risk averse, they may err on the side of taking on less risky investments for fear of the effect that greater risk could have on their future capital flows. To counteract this tendency, the optimal contract would need to involve an even higher level of incentive fees to persuade the manager to adopt the level of risk that is optimal for the investor. This effect would be even stronger for nascent funds, which endure even larger capital flow effects from gains and losses in performance (Lim et al. 2013).

Alternative Investor Criteria. Although investors frequently use past return history to evaluate money managers, they have other metrics that they can use to measure potential agents. One common metric used is the Sharpe ratio, the ratio of an investment's expected return above a benchmark to the standard deviation of this difference. Sharpe ratios are used in large part for their simplicity, although much research has identified environments in which the Sharpe ratio does not serve as a good measure of performance as well as ways in which the Sharpe ratio can be manipulated by money managers.[6]

Goetzmann, Ingersoll, Spiegel, and Welch (2004) determine the optimal investment strategy when both a market of securities and the entire continuum of option contracts on these securities are available for investment and the manager seeks to maximize the fund's Sharpe ratio. They find that out of the universe of possible investment choices, the optimal strategy is two short positions—one an out-of-the-money call and the other an out-of-the-money put—that together generate a positive immediate payment to the manager. This strategy truncates the right tail of the return probability distribution and fattens the left tail while returning a positive payoff today. In other words, with large probability, the fund generates a modestly high return, and with small probability, the fund blows up entirely. Such an approach is certainly not in the best interests of many investors, but if investors use the Sharpe ratio as an important measure of manager talent, these results imply that managers have an incentive to use this strategy. Furthermore, as suggested by Lim et al. (2013), among others, the incentive to impress investors along the dimensions they feel are important is that much stronger because of the future capital inflows that may be gained.

Investor Short-Termism

The results of Lim et al. (2013) imply that investors tend to base their investment decisions on short-term evaluation. Investors often tend to do so even when such actions may not be in their own best interests. This behavior, called investor "short-termism," is broadly accepted in the literature as simply one aspect of human nature in investing. Alfred Rappaport has written extensively on the subject in the context of corporate management, calling short-termism "a disease" for which "earnings and tracking error are the carriers" (Rappaport 2005, p. 65). Such behavior has even caused the British royal family to weigh in, with Prince Charles stating that the "current focus on quarterly capitalism is unfit for purpose" (Smith and Foley 2013).

In June 2011, the UK Secretary of State for Business, Innovation, and Skills asked John Kay to review UK equity markets and the impact of short-termism within those markets on the long-term outlook for quoted companies. Kay found that short-termism is a problem and that "the principal causes are the decline of trust and the misalignment of incentives throughout the equity investment chain" (Kay 2012, p. 9). He calls short-termism "myopic behavior" that reflects "the natural human tendency to make decisions in search of immediate gratification at the expense of future returns: decisions which we subsequently regret" (p. 14).

[6]For additional examples of how managers can manipulate their investments' Sharpe ratios, see Lo (2002) and Getmansky, Lo, and Makarov (2004).

The Generation Investment Management (2012) report titled "Sustainable Capitalism" reaches similar conclusions, calling the market "long on short and short on long" (p. 2). The report calls for several changes within the industry, recommending that asset owners embrace "ways to reshape incentives across the investment value chain" (p. 2) and that asset managers shift toward "investing for the long term and adopting incentive structures that reward such behaviour" (p. 2).

Investor short-termism is grounded in several established psychological effects, including recency (the tendency to overly focus on recent experiences) and saliency (the tendency to overweight a matter at hand and to underweight those further from one's thoughts). Lim et al. (2013) suggest further that short-termism may have an even greater impact on start-up funds, reflecting such additional effects as primacy (the tendency to overweight initial data points) and representativeness (the tendency to force new observations into categories reflected by previously encountered conventions or classifications).[7] Smith and Foley (2013) note that quantifying the effect of short-termism can be difficult, although they cite the average equity holding period as a proxy. They state that this metric in US markets has dropped from about seven years in the mid-20th century to as little as seven months in 2007 and today stands at less than two years.

In Bogle and Sullivan (2009), John Bogle, founder and former CEO of The Vanguard Group, provides similar statistics. According to Bogle, the old speculative high occurred in 1928, the year before the Great Depression began. In that year, stocks had a 140% annual turnover. As speculation decreased in the 1950s and 1960s, annual turnover dropped to about 30%. In 2006, it rose to 200%; in 2007, it was 280%; and at the time of the article's publication in 2009, it was 320%. Bogle states further that in the 1950s and 1960s, the market may have moved 2% or more in a day two to four times in a year, whereas in the approximately two years after 2007, there were more than 50 such moves.

Bogle takes a value stance on the question of short-term focus:

> So, what is driving the market now is not traditional long-term investing but untraditional and excessive short-term speculation. The market is being driven by people who are betting on future prices rather than investing with the intent to own part of a business and enjoy the returns it earns on its capital. Investment professionals—for example, pension trustees and mutual fund managers—who represent their investor-principals have been very conflicted. Many of these institutions have put their own interests—accumulating assets and earning large fees—ahead of the interests of their investors. Putting investor interests first is the way fiduciary standards are supposed to work. . . . The correctness of traditional investment principles and the legal requirement of serving principals first have not been totally

[7]See Burton and Shah (2013) for a more detailed explanation of these biases.

> abandoned, but they are certainly out of the mainstream of investing today. (Bogle and Sullivan 2009, p. 19)

To solve these problems, Bogle suggests imposing a tax on very short-term gains to help curb speculative trading, as well as supplementing the fiduciary duty of money managers with regulation enforced by powerful federal and state agencies.

The tendency of investors to focus on short-term results might force asset managers to manage for the short term in response, which might cause them to neglect the best interests of those very investors. In this circular fashion, the actions of investors may indirectly provide managers with an incentive structure that motivates them to act contrary to those investors' long-term interests. As Rappaport (2005) states:

> The fascination of investment managers with quarterly earnings . . . is perfectly rational in a market dominated by agents responsible for other people's money but also looking out for their own interests. (p. 65)

The following discourse explores this issue in a variety of contexts—corporate management, mutual funds, and hedge funds—concluding with a discussion of the consequences of this dynamic.

Short-Termism and Corporate Management. The examination of the effect of investor short-termism on corporate management largely begins with two theoretical papers by Jeremy Stein in the late 1980s. Stein (1988) posits a model of shareholder myopia that artificially depresses stock prices during a temporary period of low earnings and precipitates takeovers at unfavorable prices. Management reacts to the anticipated myopia of the firm's shareholders in a myopic fashion itself, selling off the long-term value of the firm to boost its short-term outlook.

Stein (1989) follows up that theory with a broader model of many firms in a competitive environment in which managers can reduce future earnings to increase current earnings at a discount and the market must decide how to evaluate each firm's stated earnings. This research concludes that a scenario in which management teams do not artificially inflate earnings and the market takes earnings announcements at face value could not persist, because each manager would then have an incentive to start inflating earnings. The only potential equilibrium involves managers selling the firm's long-term value to inflate current earnings, with the market rationally anticipating such behavior. That result bears repeating: Even though the market rationally anticipates the earnings inflation, managers are still better off managing earnings. This is a prisoner's dilemma–like situation in which the cooperative equilibrium—when no manager massages earnings and the market expects as much—is best for all parties but such an outcome is untenable, because each manager has a distinct incentive to defect. Consequently, each manager mortgaging the firm's future, with the market rationally anticipating this behavior, is the only possible equilibrium, even if the future sell-off occurs at a large discount to today's dollars.

The academic literature abounds with examinations of investor short-termism and its effect on corporate management. Some studies explicitly find that management acts for the short term as a result. By using conference call transcripts, Brochet, Loumioti, and Serafeim (2013) verify the relationship between short-term investor biases and short-term management decisions. The vast majority of the research in this area, however, takes as a given that management focuses on short-term horizons, rather than explicitly verifying this relationship. The consensus in the literature is that investor sentiment drives management to act this way, both for the sake of the firm's stock price and for the sake of their own jobs.[8]

Decades later, investor short-termism still garners much academic attention. Alfred Rappaport, who has written extensively on the topic, provides an example. Rappaport (2005) states that he understands the appeal of using earnings to perform discounted cash flow analyses. But earnings have limited informational power for two reasons—one, companies have considerable latitude in managing earnings, and two, earnings in one year represent a small fraction of a company's overall lifetime discounted cash flow story. Rappaport concludes that investors place too much emphasis on earnings and goes on to state that management's obsession with short-term metrics compromises shareholder value. As potential solutions for these concerns, he suggests different compensation schemes for management, including deferred compensation based on performance relative to peers, as well as new performance reporting that separates current cash flows from forward-looking accruals with certainty levels attached to future flows (Rappaport 2005).[9]

Short-Termism and Mutual Funds. As professional money management grew in scope, academic focus on investor short-termism expanded to the mutual fund industry. Ippolito's (1992) examination of this industry is the most noted work in this area. He finds that investors react significantly to the most recent period of performance but that older information has no effect on fund allocation. Furthermore, he disaggregates these flows into inflows and outflows and finds the reactions to be asymmetrical: Winning funds receive a larger increase in capital inflows than losing funds suffer in withdrawals.

Sirri and Tufano (1998) also find an asymmetry in mutual fund investor reaction to performance, stating that "fund consumers chase returns, flocking to funds with the highest recent returns, though failing to flee from

[8]See Shleifer and Vishny (1990), Bebchuk and Stole (1993), Bolton, Scheinkman, and Xiong (2006), and Bushee (1998) for additional examples. For a general survey on the topic, see Laverty (1996).

[9]See Rappaport (2011) for a broader discussion on the topic.

poor performers" (p. 1590). They find a similar asymmetry with respect to fees; investors respond to fee decreases by injecting capital, whereas fee increases cause little capital outflow. They also find that investor sensitivity to performance increases with a fund's fees. In summary, investors tend to inject money when the prospects of a fund improve, either with higher performance or lower fees, but are not quick to withdraw money when prospects diminish.

This behavior can be explained by a combination of several known psychological effects. When looking to place new money, an investor likely focuses on recent performance as a result of saliency or representativeness. Once money is placed, however, the status quo effect causes a need to feel compelled before actually making a change (Burton and Shah 2013). Consequently, investors react strongly to recent results when placing money but are slow to move those funds in the face of underperformance once those funds have been placed.

Chevalier and Ellison (1997) find similar results and dissect the data even further. They find a strong relationship between the most recent two-year returns and capital flows in the mutual fund market. Disaggregating flows into investment and divestment, they also find that minor to moderate negative performance relative to the market, defined as underperformance of 0 to 15 percentage points (pps), causes little change in capitalization, whereas underperformance of more than 15 pps causes outflows to increase dramatically. For outperformance of 0 to 15 pps, inflows increase moderately but steadily, whereas outperformance of more than 15 pps creates massive inflows for the fund.

From these results, Chevalier and Ellison then estimate the manager incentive to change risk profiles in the later months of a year given the outlook of potential inflows and outflows. Their empirical work implies, for example, that young funds that have either underperformed the market by more than 12% or outperformed it by between 0% and 10% by September have a disincentive to increase risk 50%, whereas those that have underperformed by less than 12% or outperformed by more than 10% are incentivized to increase risk. The results for older funds are directionally similar but more muted in magnitude (Chevalier and Ellison 1997).

The authors then examine whether fund managers alter the risk profiles of their portfolios as a result of the differences in inflows and outflows they expect to face. They find that, at a 1% significance level, funds alter their positions in response to the incentive to add or reduce risk implied by expected capital inflows or outflows. Put differently, they find that managers choose their investments at least in part based on their own incentives to maximize capital under management and, consequently, their long-term stream of fees, rather than following their fiduciary duty to manage the assets solely based on what is best for their investors (Chevalier and Ellison 1997).

Short-Termism and Hedge Funds. Several factors might cause capital flows in the hedge fund industry to respond to performance differently from how they do in the mutual fund industry, such as subscription periods limiting inflows and lockup and redemption periods limiting outflows. Potential investors in hedge funds may have also faced higher search costs, due to the legal advertising restrictions historically imposed on these institutions (Baquero and Verbeek 2005). The academic focus on short-termism in hedge funds, however, has been much more limited, likely because different reporting standards in this industry make empirical research more difficult to perform.

Agarwal, Daniel, and Naik (2004) examine the particulars of capital inflows to hedge funds, including how these flows relate to past performance, managerial incentives, and impediments to withdrawals. They find that money flows respond to recent performance in a convex fashion. That is, capital inflows are more sensitive to marginal performance at higher levels of performance relative to peers. They also calculate each manager's delta from a marginal dollar in investment income earned and use that as a proxy for a manager's incentive to increase returns. They find that investors place more capital with managers with higher deltas, suggesting that investors consider managerial incentives in their decisions.

Baquero and Verbeek (2005) disaggregate capital flows into investment and divestment and compare their results with prior research on the mutual fund industry. Strikingly, they find the opposite result for hedge funds than previous research found for mutual funds. They find that inflows are sensitive to long-run overperformance, whereas outflows respond immediately to underperformance. They also find that these relationships are linear in nature, whereas previous research found such relationships, especially for positive performance, to be convex. They posit the extensive up-front search cost involved in vetting a hedge fund and its managers as an explanation for the slow reaction to recent outperformance, whereas they reason that withdrawing money after a period of underperformance requires much less time to comfortably execute.

Consequences of Investor Short-Termism. The research on firm management, mutual funds, and hedge funds has shown that investors and general stakeholders focus on short time horizons in their agent evaluation. In a seminal paper in behavioral finance, De Long, Shleifer, Summers, and Waldmann (1990) highlight one issue that could arise as a result of this short-termism. Before this work, stalwarts of the efficient market hypothesis (EMH) had long maintained that markets required only one rational actor to maintain efficiency because any irrational actors in the market would have their irrational trades counteracted by the rational actor, who would reap the rewards once market prices returned to fundamental values. These proponents argued that this outcome would hold true regardless of how many irrational investors existed in the marketplace because the rational investor would always just counter their positions and simply wait until the market returned to form (Burton and Shah 2013).

De Long et al. (1990), however, show that when investors face finite time horizons, fully countering these irrational trades may not be in the investors' best interests. Their model involves a set of rational investors who know the fundamental value of a given asset and another set of investors who irrationally believe the asset to have a different value. All investors make their investment decisions in one period and then liquidate their holdings in the next in an overlapping generations framework. Consequently, rational investors can take only so large a position against irrational movements of the market for fear that the market might move against them even further and might not correct before they are forced to liquidate. This possibility limits the extent to which a manager can invest to benefit his or her investors, given the risk of further incorrect market movements against the manager's position in the short term and the consequent redemptions that may result.

According to Agnew (2012), the investor tendency toward short-termism has been amplified by the experience of the financial crisis of 2008. Prior to the crisis, capital inflows were large and hedge funds were able to dictate favorable terms. When the crisis hit, however, liquidity dried up and many funds imposed restrictions to keep investors from withdrawing their assets. This strategy changed the perception of hedge funds in investors' minds from vehicles that provide outsized returns with high liquidity to institutions in which one's capital might get locked up. This shift in investor sentiment forced hedge funds as a group to move toward more liquid terms. Less than a third of all hedge funds offered monthly liquidity or better in 2008, compared with 58% in 2013. In 2011, fewer than 7% of funds offered liquidity less frequently than quarterly, whereas about 25% did in 2008. Agnew finds that this shift toward greater liquidity has cost hedge funds the ability to deliver the same performance. Overall, she finds the current investor demands for high liquidity, high returns, and low volatility to be incompatible with one another.

Frazzini, Kabiller, and Pedersen (2013) describe one possible way to avoid the effects of investor short-termism, using Warren Buffett's Berkshire Hathaway as a model for discussion. They examine Berkshire's history from 1976 to 2011 and find that it achieved a Sharpe ratio of 0.76, higher than that of any stock or mutual fund with at least 30 years of history from 1926 to 2011. Berkshire returned an annualized 19.0% in excess of the T-bill rate for 1976–2011, compared with an annualized excess return of 6.1% for the general market. Berkshire's volatility, however, was also higher, at 24.9% versus 15.8% for the overall market. This volatility led to some large drawdown periods, including a 76% underperformance compared with the market from

1998 to 2000 as the tech bubble was building; during this period, Berkshire lost 44% of its market value while the stock market gained 32%. But these drawdowns did not bring about the demise of Berkshire Hathaway, although similar losses have undone other large funds in the past.

Frazzini et al. (2013) attribute this outcome not only to Buffett's stellar ability as an investor but also to Berkshire's unique corporate structure. According to the authors:

> We find that both public and private companies contribute to Buffett's performance, but the portfolio of public stocks performed better, suggesting that Buffett's skill is mostly in stock selection. Why then does Buffett rely heavily on private companies as well, including insurance and reinsurance businesses? One reason might be that this structure provides a steady source of financing, allowing him to leverage his stock selection ability. Indeed, we find that 36% of Buffett's liabilities consist of insurance float with an average cost below the T-Bill rate. (p. 4)

They liken collecting insurance premiums up front and later paying out claims to taking out and repaying a loan, and they find Berkshire's cost of capital in this context to be more than three percentage points lower than the average T-bill rate (Frazzini et al. 2013).

This permanent base of capital allows Berkshire Hathaway to avoid the whims of investor sentiment, immunizing it from the vicious cycle of redemptions that has forced other large funds to unwind quickly. Since Berkshire's inception, several other hedge funds have followed its lead. Many have launched reinsurance companies, including Moore Capital in 1999 (Mider 2013); Greenlight in 2004 (Davidoff 2012); and SAC, Third Point, and Paulson—all after 2010 (Mider 2013). Others have launched other publicly traded vehicles, such as the two publicly traded REITs created by Pine River Capital Management—Two Harbors, which began in 2009, and Silver Bay, which had its IPO in 2012 (St. Anthony 2013).

The Banking Industry and the Financial Crisis of 2008

The previous two sections explored the asset management industry, including a discussion of the direct incentives that compensation contracts provide to managers, as well as one of the indirect incentives that investor short-termism provides to those same managers. This section turns the focus to another important area of the financial system: the banking industry. It uses the financial crisis of 2008, an important event from recent history that illuminated many of the principal–agent problems endemic to this industry, as a case study and analyzes the numerous instances of misaligned incentives that contributed to the crisis.

The complexity of the banking industry creates an environment that is ripe for potential incentive conflicts. In the run-up to the financial crisis, bank employees, both those executing the trades to purchase securities and those managing the traders, often faced conflicts between the incentives created by their compensation contracts and their duty to the shareholders of their companies. The government certainly faced tension between its duty to represent taxpayer interests and its stance of not interfering with private industry. And the bailouts themselves forged a new principal–agent relationship between bank managers and the taxpayers whose money was used to stabilize their institutions. The myriad interconnected relationships among the various parties involved, combined with the density of relevant information in each transaction, provided a fertile breeding ground for principal–agent issues. Furthermore, the amount of money involved amplified each individual's incentives significantly, making them that much more difficult to ignore. The following discussion reviews the literature on these relationship pairs and the principal–agent problems that existed within them.

Bank Employees as Agents for Shareholders. The classic principal–agent relationship, that of worker or manager as agent for the firm owner, played its part in the events of the financial crisis. Many have attributed much of the responsibility for the crisis to bank employees, stating that compensation contracts structured incentives in such a way as to misalign them with those of shareholders and promote actions that did not forward the best interests of the banks themselves. Being closest to the decisions that accumulated risk on bank balance sheets, bank traders have been chastised for sacrificing long-term firm value to line their own pockets. Management, meanwhile, has received similar blame for its oversight—or lack thereof.

- *Traders as agents for shareholders.* The crisis literature is nearly unanimous on the existence of principal–agent problems in the relationship between bank traders and the shareholders of the banks they represented. Crotty's (2009) scathing piece sets the tone for the discussion. According to Crotty, traders received incentive compensation based on profits created in a given year, regardless of the risk these trades created for the banks in future years. Crotty cites as evidence AIG's Financial Products division, which lost $40.5 billion in 2008 but whose employees received a total of $220 million in bonuses for that year, which averages to more than $500,000 per employee. Under this incentive scheme, Crotty concludes, taking excessive risk during a bubble actually represents rational behavior, even if the individual trader knows his or her actions are likely to contribute to a crash in the intermediate future.

Kirkpatrick (2009) also posits a misalignment between trader compensation and firm incentives. He states that traders, especially senior ones, generally have unlimited upside to their bonuses, whereas the downside is floored at zero, with any losses borne by the bank and its shareholders. He makes two suggestions to cure this defect. The first is to defer bonus compensation subject to future clawback to better align outcomes with the long-term interests of shareholders. The second is to incorporate the amount of capital put at risk into employee performance targets, which some banks do, although most do not.

Crotty (2009) delves further into the relationship between trader compensation and firm incentives, going into detail on the subject of collateralized debt obligation (CDO) sales. He states that when bank traders found the safest tranches of mortgage-backed securities hard to sell, they kept those tranches on their banks' balance sheets and sold the remaining portions to boost bonuses from additional sales. Crotty states that this behavior persisted despite the fact that it put unhedged risk on the balance sheet, citing the following now-famous quote from Citigroup CEO Charles Prince:

> When the music stops, in terms of liquidity, things will be complicated. But as long as the music is playing, you've got to get up and dance. We're still dancing. (pp. 568–569)

Crotty (2009) then dives deeper into the complexity inherent in these securities and includes a description of CDOs, CDO-squareds, and higher-power CDOs. According to Crotty, these securities are so complex that it can take a powerful computer several days to price a single CDO via black box simulation models. He believes this complexity gives sellers of these instruments an informational advantage over the buyers of these securities, creating, in effect, a new and separate principal–agent problem. Whoever prices the security can, in Crotty's judgment, manipulate the statistical models to produce a price that reflects his or her interests, while the buyer sees only the subset of information that the seller chooses to present.

Alan Blinder, a former vice chairman of the Federal Reserve, describes in a 2009 *Wall Street Journal* opinion piece how traders' compensation structures incentivize them to take big bets, with the downside being absorbed by "other people's money" (p. A15). According to Blinder, the same is true for CEOs, whereas the shareholders, those whose interests they represent, want to take many fewer of these risky bets. He attributes the evolution of these arrangements to changes in the ownership structure of banks over the past few decades. When banks were partnerships employing the partners' capital, the partners were much more averse to giving traders the liberty to take large bets (with the partners' money). With the shift toward stockholder-owned corporations, the management and ownership groups separated, creating a divergence in incentives and thereby causing a change in behavior. Blinder describes hedge funds as hybrid structures that invest partner money in addition to other people's money and cites this arrangement as an important reason why these funds bet far less significantly on mortgage-related securities before the crisis.

Blinder (2009) considers it to be the role of government to abolish compensation practices that misalign employee and shareholder incentives, but he adds that when this approach was tried two decades ago in an initiative that he was a part of, it failed miserably. Instead, he blames boards of directors, stating that these bodies are supposed to represent the interests of the shareholders but instead often reflect those of management. According to Blinder:

> The unhappy (but common) combination of coziness and drowsiness in corporate boardrooms must end. As one concrete manifestation, boards should abolish go-for-broke incentives and change compensation practices to align the interests of shareholders and employees better. . . . The problems are many and complex, and the government's to-do list is not only long but also a political minefield. Yet fixing compensation incentives does not require any government action. It can be done by financial companies, tomorrow. Too bad they didn't do it yesterday. (p. A15)

■ *Management as agent for shareholders.* Although the literature presents near unanimity on the principal–agent problems caused by the incentive structures of bank traders, the verdict on management incentive structures is much more mixed. Soon after the crisis, several opinion pieces came out stating emphatically and unequivocally that compensation structures for bank CEOs caused them to act counter to the banks' interests. John Bogle, in his interview with *Financial Analysts Journal* editor Rodney Sullivan (Bogle and Sullivan 2009), states that the asymmetry inherent in management's joining in the firm's upside during good times without forfeiting those proceeds when downside risks are realized cannot continue to go unacknowledged as a major issue. He calls for government regulation as the cure.

Crotty (2009) again provides a scathing viewpoint, citing such statistics as those regarding Merrill Lynch's chief executives, who were paid $240 million in performance-based compensation from 1997 to 2008 despite the fact that Merrill's losses in 2007 and 2008 wiped out all previous earnings reported by the firm over that time frame. Crotty's discussion of the complexity of the relevant securities further implies that mark-to-model practices afforded management an additional layer of private information that it could use to further its own interests at the expense of shareholders.

As time passed, however, researchers performed in-depth empirical analysis, and the results became more mixed. Kirkpatrick (2009) examines the remuneration policies of banks to determine whether management had incentives to take excessive risk. He finds that some bank CEOs received most of their compensation in the form of stock or options, whereas others received mainly short-term compensation. As of 2006, European banks paid 24% of CEO compensation in fixed salary, 36% in cash bonuses, and 40% in long-term incentives. In contrast, a study of six US banks found that salary made up only 4% to 6% of top executive compensation, with stock compensation reaching very high levels. Kirkpatrick cites an example of one bank in particular that leaned strongly toward long-term compensation, requiring the CEO to hold shares worth five times the previous three years' average cash component. From these data, he concludes that management incentives to take risks varied considerably across banks. He also cites the finding that banks that failed tended to have CEOs with higher stock holdings, whereas the banks that survived had higher incentives to take risks, implying that the incentive alignment may not have mattered anyway.

Kirkpatrick (2009) also gives an overview of the contribution of corporate governance structure to the financial crisis. For example, he says board members faltered in their responsibility to represent shareholders, both in failing to create systems that would cause information about risk exposure to reach senior management and in approving strategy decisions without instituting the appropriate systems to monitor their implementation. He finds that firms whose management exerted more control over their balance sheet, liquidity, and capital typically performed better during the crisis.

Chesney, Stromberg, and Wagner (2010) consider bank CEO compensation as a derivative instrument, using the related terminology: delta, the sensitivity of the CEO's compensation to the value of the bank's stock, and vega, the sensitivity of the CEO's compensation to the volatility of the bank's stock price. The higher a CEO's delta, the greater the alignment between his or her incentives and those of the bank's shareholders; the higher a CEO's vega, the greater the alignment between his or her incentives and those of the bank's optionholders or, equivalently, the greater his or her incentive to take risks. Chesney et al. find that bank write-downs are positively associated with the CEO's vega, implying that banks whose CEOs had a higher incentive to take risks performed worse. They also find that write-downs are negatively associated with the CEO's delta, implying that banks whose CEOs' incentives had greater alignment with those of the shareholders performed better. They find, however, that the vega effect dominates the delta effect quantitatively. The positive relationship between bank write-downs and vega also strengthens when alternative versions of vega are used, such as the sensitivity of the CEO's wealth to discrete changes or jumps in risk—that is, to changes in the nature of the risk taken.

Fahlenbrach and Stulz (2011), in contrast, report directionally opposite results. They find some evidence that banks whose CEOs' interests were more closely aligned with those of shareholders actually performed worse during the crisis. They also find that banks whose CEO compensation packages were more sensitive to stock volatility (or, equivalently, had a higher vega) did not suffer worse stock returns during the crisis. Furthermore, they find that bank returns during the crisis are negatively related to the dollar incentives represented by the CEO's equity compensation. Lastly, they find that bank CEOs did not liquidate their equity in advance of the crisis, causing them to lose much of their wealth during it, in line with the fate of the shareholders they represented. The authors conclude that these findings are inconsistent with the view that CEOs led banks to take on excessive risk as a result of their own incentives and in spite of those of shareholders.

Bailouts. The advent of the government bailout programs created a separate, yet less classically obvious, principal–agent relationship. When the Troubled Asset Relief Program (TARP) was signed into law, the government agreed to use taxpayer dollars to prop up financial institutions to avoid the systemic risks that would result from their collapse. As steward of the taxpayers' funds, the government implicitly took on the responsibility of using those assets judiciously. As such, it bore the burden of funding only those institutions with the greatest systemic importance so as to maximize the trade-off between spending taxpayer dollars and reducing the negative externalities that might be borne by the public if the financial system were to collapse.

The structure of the bailout programs itself created a second, related principal–agent relationship. Because some banks had flexibility about whether to apply for aid, any misalignment between the banks' interests and those of the taxpayers could result in a misuse of those bailout funds. Furthermore, to the extent that it had been assumed that the government would bail out systemically important institutions if large risks turned against them, the banks were implicitly acting as agents of the taxpayer while making those risky decisions all along.

■ *Lessons from the Japanese crisis.* Some research has shown striking similarities between the Japanese banking crisis of the late 1990s and the financial collapse of 2008. Iwatsubo (2007) examines the behavior in the 1990s of Japanese banks, which shifted lending from other sectors to real estate even in the face of declining land prices. He cites moral hazard as the explanation, describing the problem as "gambling for resurrection" (p. 167). Essentially, poorly capitalized banks used the backstop of the deposit insurance system as a reason to choose a riskier asset portfolio in an effort to become competitive again.

Iwatsubo then takes this analysis one step further, showing empirically that the decision to increase or decrease risk in response to a decline in capital depends on the initial franchise value of the bank. High-valued banks decrease risk to avoid falling into insolvency, whereas low-valued banks increase risk to try to become competitive in the marketplace again. The put option inherent in the deposit insurance system again serves as a backstop against this increased risk (Iwatsubo 2007).

Furthermore, Iwatsubo (2007) creates a theoretical model reflecting the banks' incentives and analyzes how capital adequacy requirements and capital injections by government affect the banks' incentives to assume risk. He finds that a prospective future capital requirement incentivizes banks to assume more risk today as a result of the expectation of increased future capital costs, whereas a prospective future capital injection program has the opposite effect because of the expectation of reduced future capital costs. He also finds that, empirically, as banks approached the capital adequacy requirement in the 1990s, they simply issued more subordinated debt to ease the capital restriction and bet harder on real estate to try to become competitive again. The additional subordinated debt issuance eased the capital crunch, but the increased leverage on the real estate bets simply increased the problem of nonperforming loans.

Other research has directly compared the US financial crisis with that of Japan a decade earlier. Hoshi and Kashyap (2010) develop a framework to evaluate the US government's role post-crisis, using the role of the Japanese government in the Japanese banking crisis of the 1990s and the resulting outcome for comparison. They find a number of similarities between the two crises and identify eight lessons that the US government should have learned from Japan's experience. Many of these lessons involve the potential principal–agent problem inherent in allowing banks free choice over whether or not to receive assistance. With this autonomy, the banks essentially act as agents for the taxpayers, deciding whether or not to accept funds to stem a systemic collapse and avoid the resulting negative externalities that taxpayers might face (Hoshi and Kashyap 2010).

The authors posit that a potentially failing bank may have a stronger incentive to refuse assistance than the taxpayers would like, for two reasons. First, accepting assistance serves as a negative signal indicating the bank's inability to receive additional funding in private markets. Second, exchanging new securities that sit above common equity in the capital structure creates a debt overhang problem for the existing shareholders. These two factors do not affect the taxpayers' willingness to aid the banks but do enter into a given bank's decision making. The lesson as stated here involves incorporating the possibility that banks will reject assistance from the aid programs in such a way that banks' incentives to accept or reject assistance are aligned with those of the taxpayers (Hoshi and Kashyap 2010).

They find further that the Japanese government program did not adequately tie assistance to credible inspection programs. They posit that this omission was intended to remove the potential negative signal associated with accepting aid, but ironically, the banks hesitated to accept aid anyway. Consequently, the 1998 program was too small. A similar program the following year did involve inspections, and the authors provide evidence that this program was more successful in inducing lending by the recipient banks than the predecessor program was. Regulators, however, did not force banks to clean up their nonperforming loans, and this omission resulted in suboptimal outcomes (Hoshi and Kashyap 2010).

Several of the other lessons also involve principal–agent issues inherent in the banks' ability to push back against the reforms. Cited failings include forcing the banks to take more aid than they preferred as well as not nationalizing the most troubled banks and forcing them to unwind. Hoshi and Kashyap (2010) evaluate the US government's post-crisis policies and find that, although it is too early to assess the effect of policies addressing half of the eight lessons they specify, only one of those lessons was heeded by the government, whereas at least three were clearly ignored, including the two listed above.

■ *Application to the US crisis.* Hoshi and Kashyap's (2010) research raises two key questions regarding the government's and banks' roles as agents for the taxpayers: (1) Did the parameters of the Capital Purchase Program (CPP) eliminate the potential adverse selection problem in which the wrong banks (from society's point of view) opt in, and (2) did the Treasury approve the banks whose financial distress costs were the highest? In response to this research, Bayazitova and Shivdasani (2012) assess the decisions of banks as a result of their incentives in the marketplace. This study addresses the issue of the banks, as agents of society, potentially receiving government aid not for the protection of a given bank's shareholders but as a result of the externalities that the bank's failure would cause for society because of its systemic importance in the economy.

They find the answer to both questions above to be yes. Banks that did not apply for the CPP tended to have stronger capital ratios, more stable funding profiles, and higher asset quality than those that did apply, whereas those that were accepted into the program were larger and posed greater systemic risk. The authors also find that banks that were approved for CPP funds but rejected them received little boost to equity valuations. They conclude that the adverse signaling and debt overhang concerns raised by Hoshi and Kashyap (2010) did not prevent the weakest banks from participating in the buyout program (Bayazitova and Shivdasani 2012).

The authors, however, do find evidence that management's personal incentives may have played a role in bank behavior. TARP placed compensation limits on the banks' management, and the political climate around the passage of TARP was such that many anticipated further political interference in management compensation for banks that accepted TARP funds. Management's incentive to disassociate from TARP increased notably with the passage of H.R. 1586, which placed a 90% tax on all employee bonuses given by institutions that received at least $5 billion of TARP assistance.

First, Bayazitova and Shivdasani (2012) examine the banks' decision whether to accept or reject CPP. They find that banks with CEO compensation over the TARP limit were more likely to reject TARP and that this likelihood to reject increased significantly with management compensation, as did the probability that a bank would exit TARP once in it. These findings suggest that management, appointed as agent for the shareholders and acting as surrogate agent for the taxpayers, may have instead acted in its own best interests rather than in the best interests of the principals it was supposed to represent.

Bayazitova and Shivdasani (2012) also touch on the potential conflict between the two agency roles of the government as a result of TARP. According to the authors, through the FDIC guarantee on deposits, the government essentially owned a claim on bank assets that was senior to several layers of debt and all layers of equity. Consequently, much of the capital structure would have to falter before regulators forced the bank to raise additional capital or seized bank assets. But the insertion of a government-owned layer of preferred equity meant that only the common equity layer remained as a buffer to protect taxpayers before regulators would have to act. If the market had perceived this situation as an increase in risk, the market price should have reacted, which is exactly what the authors find. Using two proxies for the thickness of the common equity cushion—the common equity component of the Tier 1 capital ratio and the tangible common equity ratio—they find that both became correlated with stock returns only after the CPP infusions took place. They conclude that this finding is consistent with the view that markets perceived a shift in government incentives under the CPP and an associated additional risk in having a thin layer of common equity capital. By providing this new capital injection meant to help banks, the government shifted its own incentives in a way that hurt banks with a small common equity layer relative to those with a larger buffer.

In a Hoover Institution journal piece, Richard Epstein (2013) discusses a more current consequence of the government's entering the capital structure of private firms as agent for the taxpayers. In 2008, the Federal Housing Finance Agency (FHFA), acting in its authority as conservator of Fannie Mae and Freddie Mac, struck a deal with the US Treasury that stabilized the two institutions in exchange for preferred stock amounting to $1 billion. According to Epstein, the Housing and Economic Recovery Act (HERA) gave the Treasury broad discretion as to the terms and conditions attached to that stock, but it also directed the government to guide Fannie and Freddie toward becoming stable, private, shareholder-owned companies. In August 2012, the FHFA and the Treasury signed an amendment that provided the Treasury with a full sweep of Fannie's and Freddie's earnings as interest on the taxpayers' investment.

Several lawsuits have been filed as a result. Based on these filings, Epstein (2013) lists three ways in which the government is alleged to have conflicts of interest in its role as agent for the taxpayers. The first involves a conflict of interest for the FHFA, which has a fiduciary duty to act on behalf of the Fannie and Freddie shareholders in its role as conservator but also has a duty to act on behalf of the taxpayers in its role as part of the government. The second pertains to an alleged violation of the Administrative Procedure Act and involves a conflict of interest within the government between its duty to act on behalf of the taxpayers as owners of Fannie and Freddie and its duty to all parties involved to administer HERA according to its specified terms, including guiding Fannie and Freddie toward private ownership. The third revolves around an improper use of the law of takings and involves a conflict between the government's role as agent of the taxpayers and its duty to provide just compensation when it forcibly removes private property. Implicit in the last allegation rests the idea that usurping all profits from lower levels of the capital structure is tantamount to taking the property itself.

One question raised by a governmental policy of responding to systemic risk is how to accurately estimate the systemic risk of a bank. One popular proxy for systemic risk has been bank size, as evidenced by the popular slogan for the government bailout programs, "too big to fail." Zhou (2009) uses one previously invented measure—PAO, or the probability that at least one other bank becomes distressed upon the given bank's failure—and invents two other measures of the systemic risk or importance of a given bank: SII, or the expected number of bank failures in the banking system upon the given bank's failure, and VI, or the probability of the given bank's failure given that at least one other failure in the system occurs. He finds that size does not necessarily correlate well with systemic importance and, therefore, should not automatically be taken as an accurate measure of systemic risk. He posits instead using a bank's leverage ratio as a potential tool to identify banks with high systemic risk.

Crotty (2009) also identifies a principal–agent problem within the US government, specifically in former Goldman Sachs CEO Henry Paulson's acting as secretary of the Treasury. He highlights Paulson's decision to let Lehman Brothers go under and his subsequent actions to save AIG, from which Goldman Sachs received $12.9 billion in taxpayer money as a result of its transactions with the insurance giant. Crotty insinuates that Paulson's past relationship with Goldman Sachs entered into his decision making on this issue, and he further concludes that this arrangement allowed banks to gamble with a public money backstop, incentivizing them to take large bets as they participated in upside outcomes while shifting the burden to taxpayers on the downside.

■ *Analysis of government policy.* According to John Bogle, over time, financial markets have reached the point of privatization of profits with public assumption of risk, whether through government-sponsored enterprises, such as Fannie Mae and Freddie Mac, or through bailouts of the banking system. In a sense, when governmental policy is to bail out banks that fail during a crisis, the banks become agents acting on behalf of the taxpayers, who are assuming the risk of the banks' actions. Bogle states that such a system, in which government assumes the risk but does not take a strong regulatory or ownership role, cannot persist (Bogle and Sullivan 2009).

Poole (2009) posits an interesting market-based solution. He recommends regulation that would require every bank above a size threshold to maintain 10% of its liabilities as 10-year uncollateralized notes that are subordinated to all other debt obligations, so the bank would have to refinance one-tenth of this debt every year. If a particular bank could not refinance this debt in a given year, it would have to shrink its balance sheet by 10%. This restructuring would be managed by the bank itself rather than the government, mitigating potential principal–agent problems. Moreover, in the event of another bailout, this layer of the capital structure would provide an additional cushion before taxpayers suffered losses.

Rating Agencies as Agents for the Market. Another principal–agent problem examined in the crisis literature involves the rating agencies as agents for the market. As independent arbiters, these agencies are tasked with rating various financial instruments as accurately and objectively as possible. As Crotty (2009) argues, however, these parties receive fee revenue for each instrument rated and face no recourse if the securities or loans do not perform later. Therefore, the rating agencies' incentive was simply to maximize deal flow rather than optimize the quality of their output. According to Crotty, competition among the rating agencies exacerbated this problem because banks merely shopped around for the highest rating provider.

Kirkpatrick (2009) also analyzes the rating agencies' role in the financial crisis. He cites the concentration of banks that represent the rating agencies' customer base as creating a potential conflict of interest in which the agencies must appease their customers to get repeat business. Furthermore, he addresses the fact that agencies engage in discussions with banks about how to structure an instrument to get the desired rating, likening this scenario to an auditor auditing his or her own work; the agencies are rating a security that they themselves helped to design.

Kotecha, Ryan, and Weinberger (2010) make a similar argument—that market forces place downward pressure on ratings accuracy as a result of the "ratings shopping" behavior cited by Crotty (2009). They examine the ratings environment closely and conclude that simply increasing ratings transparency, as previous governmental acts have attempted to do, cannot fix the problem: The underlying compensation model must also be changed. They propose a new structure in which rating costs are deducted from issuance proceeds and yearly interest payments cover annual reevaluation of the ratings.

Other Principal–Agent Relationships. Crotty (2009) extends his argument involving fee income to other parties in the crisis, including the mortgage brokers who sold the loans, the investment bankers who packaged them, and the banks that serviced them. Crotty argues that all of these parties were incentivized to maximize flow rather than quality. He also addresses the obscurity involved in the CDO market, stating that this obscurity gives the banks selling these securities another layer of private information in deals with counterparties. Because the banks' objective is to maximize flow, they have an incentive to not provide counterparties with the entire truth in these transactions.

As Timiraos and Zibel (2013) point out, government regulation has attempted to address this issue by forcing banks to keep 5% of these securities on their balance sheets so that they have some "skin in the game," but individuals on both the bank side and the consumer advocate side oppose such rules. Both groups agree that the new rules would be much more complex than the old ones and would, therefore, raise costs both for lenders and for consumers.

Conclusion

As the study of market entities within economics grew ever more granular, academic focus shifted from industries to firms and then to individual parties within firms. Consequently, the issue of competing incentives within cooperative arrangements came to the fore. Simultaneously, economists began studying the behavior of individuals before and after entering into risk-sharing agreements. Eventually, these two paths merged into the study of agency theory, from which the concept of the principal–agent problem was born.

The principal is one who delegates work to another, known as the agent, who performs the task on the principal's behalf. When the agent has an ethical obligation to act in a way that reflects the principal's incentives but the agent's own incentives lie on an orthogonal path, the agent is faced with a conflict between an ethical imperative and his or her personal interests. It is not difficult to see how the financial system could provide a fertile breeding ground for principal–agent issues, given its interconnected nature and the risk-sharing features of the products often sold within it.

Organizations such as CFA Institute have developed codes of ethics to guide professionals in finance and to set expectations for ethical behavior in such situations. Reflection upon such behavior and how successful the industry as a whole has been in achieving its ethical goals has rarely been more important than it is at the current time. Financial products and relationships have become so complex and interwoven that discerning ethical actions from irresponsible behavior is increasingly difficult, as demonstrated by the recent financial crisis, which threatened to bring down the entire financial system. Investors as well as the general public have noticed, as several recent surveys have shown, that trust both of and within the financial markets has reached frighteningly low levels.

This review has aimed to summarize the existing literature on topics germane to the principal–agent problem. It split the discussion into two parts, focusing first on investment management and then shifting to the banking industry. It began with a broad view of compensation schemes for asset managers in the contexts of hedge funds and mutual funds. These compensation structures directly provide managers with incentives that, if misaligned with those of the investors, can lead to conflicts with those managers' fiduciary duty. These contracts often have a management component that provides revenue in the form of a percentage of assets under management, as well as an incentive fee equivalent to a share of the upside return. The latter component has often been blamed for incentivizing managers to take on too much risk as a result of its embedded call optionality. Research that examines this issue in a static, or one-period, context has concluded as such. But work that examines this question in a dynamic context has sometimes found that incentive fees actually cause managers to take on too little risk. From the manager's point of view, the downside risk of losing money and thereby not growing the fund over time—or, worse, facing redemptions—often outweighs the upside risk of additional incentive proceeds because of the immense stream of future management fees on existing and additional capital that is at stake.

The discourse then moved to investor "short-termism," or the tendency for investors to focus on short-term performance rather than on the long-term outlook that represents their best interests. Investor short-termism has been well documented in its effect on corporate governance, where short-term thinking by stockholders causes management to sacrifice the long-term interests of the company for small short-term gains. This same phenomenon has been observed in the much newer field of asset management. Such behavior by investors indirectly provides managers with an incentive to manage for the short term, thereby misaligning the managers' incentives with those of the very investors whose assets they are managing. The theoretical research suggests that the effect of such behavior can profoundly hamper managers' ability to achieve optimal risk and return targets for their investors. Consequently, many asset managers have sought out sources of capital with longer lock-up periods, thus launching publicly traded entities to provide more stable capital bases and avoid the misaligned incentives that investor short-termism can create.

Finally, the discussion shifted to the banking industry, focusing on the myriad principal–agent relationships that catalyzed the financial crisis of 2008. Research on the compensation structures of senior executives at banks is mixed, whereas most research on the incentives of the traders and others more directly involved in the decision making points to these incentives as reasons for the increased risk on bank balance sheets. The role of the government in the crisis was also examined, with several key financial figures weighing in on changes the government must make to the current market environment to prevent such problems from recurring. The literature also offers considerable criticism of the compensation methods for the rating agencies, claiming that their pay schemes incentivize them to sacrifice accuracy for speed and to shade their ratings up to benefit their clients.

The problems, as outlined in this work, are well known, but the question that remains is who will act to solve them in the future. On their own, members of the financial profession are realizing that it is not enough to just avoid conflicts or manage their own conflicts responsibly. A more sustainable financial system requires a more trustworthy reputation, not just for individuals but for the industry. Where there has at times been a leadership void, the financial crisis has prompted CFA Institute and other organizations to take a more active role to (1) better align interests so that the economic purpose of finance can be realized and (2) speak out to discourage poor business practices. By finding ways to cultivate a more ethical culture in the finance industry, we can together shape a better future of finance.

I would like to thank CFA Institute for the opportunity to write this literature review and the members of its staff, including Rodney Sullivan, CFA, Larry Siegel, and Barbara Petitt, CFA, for their hard work in helping get this document to completion. I am also grateful to Vaishali Shah, Bruce MacDonald, Adam Oestreich, Colin Teichholtz, and Maxim Engers for all of their thoughtful comments and suggestions. All remaining errors are my own.

This qualifies for 2 CE credits, inclusive of 2 SER credits.

Bibliography

Agarwal, Vikas, Naveen Daniel, and Narayan Naik. 2004. "Flows, Performance, and Managerial Incentives in Hedge Funds." EFA 2003 Annual Conference Paper No. 501 (July):1–44 (http://papers.ssrn.com/sol3/papers.cfm?abstract_id=424369).

> "This paper investigates the determinants of money-flows, nature of managerial incentives, behavior of investors, and drivers of performance in the hedge fund industry. It examines performance-flow relation and finds that funds with good recent performance, greater managerial incentives, and lower impediments to capital withdrawals experience higher money-flows. It also analyzes how current money-flows relate to future performance and finds that larger funds with greater inflows are associated with poorer future performance, a result consistent with decreasing returns to scale. It also finds that funds with greater managerial incentives are associated with superior future performance, justifying investors' preference for funds with higher managerial incentives." (Abstract)

Agarwal, Vikas, Naveen Daniel, and Narayan Naik. 2009. "Role of Managerial Incentives and Discretion in Hedge Fund Performance." *Journal of Finance*, vol. 64, no. 5 (October):2221–2256.

> "Using a comprehensive hedge fund database, we examine the role of managerial incentives and discretion in hedge fund performance. Hedge funds with greater managerial incentives, proxied by the delta of the option-like incentive fee contracts, higher levels of managerial ownership, and the inclusion of high-water mark provisions in the incentive contracts, are associated with superior performance. The incentive fee percentage rate by itself does not explain performance. We also find that funds with a higher degree of managerial discretion, proxied by longer lockup, notice, and redemption periods, deliver superior performance. These results are robust to using alternative performance measures and controlling for different data-related biases." (p. 2221)

Agnew, Harriet. 2012. "Investor Short-Termism Is the Bane of Hedge Funds." *Financial News* (1 October): http://www.efinancialnews.com/story/2012-10-01/investor-short-termism-bane-of-hedge-funds.

> Agnew examines the ways investor short-termism has changed as a result of the financial crisis as well as the effect it has had on hedge funds. She discusses the current investor mandate and provides her opinion on its tendency to depress fund returns.

Arrow, Kenneth. 1971. *Essays in the Theory of Risk-Bearing*. Chicago: Markham Publishing.

This work contains a compilation of Arrow's contributions to the "decision-making under uncertainty" subdiscipline of economics.

Baquero, Guillermo. and Marno Verbeek. 2005. "A Portrait of Hedge Fund Investors: Flows, Performance, and Smart Money." ERIM Report Series Reference No. ERS-2005-068-F&A (November):1–53 (http://papers.ssrn.com/sol3/papers.cfm?abstract_id=851625).

"We explore the flow-performance interrelation by explicitly separating the investment and divestment decisions of hedge fund investors. The results show that different determinants and evaluation horizons underlie both decisions. While money inflows are sensitive to past long-run performance, outflows exhibit an immediate and sustained response to past performance in the short run. As a consequence, the shape of the flow-performance relation differs depending on the time horizon being analyzed. We find a weaker flow-performance relation for winning funds at quarterly horizons compared to annual horizons, which may explain why quarterly persistence in hedge fund performance is not competed away. Indeed, we also find evidence that most investors are unable to exploit the persistence of the winners. Conversely, investors are fast and successful in deallocating from the persistent losers, ensuring a disciplining mechanism for low quality funds. Further, our findings do not support the existence of smart money." (p. 2)

Bayazitova, Dinara, and Anil Shivdasani. 2012. "Assessing TARP." *Review of Financial Studies*, vol. 25, no. 2 (February):377–407.

"We study the government equity infusions into banks under the Capital Purchase Program (CPP) of the Troubled Asset Relief Program (TARP). Strong banks opted out of CPP, and equity infusions were provided to banks that posed systemic risk and faced high financial distress costs but had strong asset quality. Concerns over executive compensation led banks to reject CPP infusions and exit the program. CPP infusions did not have meaningful certification effects, but the subsequent stress tests conducted for the major banks had significant certification effects. CPP equity infusions increased investor expectations regarding future regulatory interventions in the banking sector." (p. 377)

Bebchuk, Lucian Arye, and Lars A. Stole. 1993. "Do Short-Term Objectives Lead to Under- or Overinvestment in Long-Term Projects?" *Journal of Finance*, vol. 48, no. 2 (June):719–730.

"We examine managerial investment decisions in the presence of imperfect information and short-term managerial objectives. Prior research has argued that such an environment induces managers to underinvest in long-run projects. We show that short-term objectives and imperfect information may also lead to overinvestment, and we identify how the direction of the distortion depends upon the type of informational imperfection present. When investors cannot observe the level of investment in the long-run project, suboptimal investment will be induced. When investors can observe investment but not its productivity, however, overinvestment will occur." (p. 719)

Blinder, Alan S. 2009. "Crazy Compensation and the Crisis." *Wall Street Journal* (28 May):A15.

Blinder's opinion piece in the *Wall Street Journal* discusses the compensation structure for members of banks on Wall Street and how he thinks these structures contributed to the big bets that caused the financial crisis.

Bogle, John C., and Rodney N. Sullivan. 2009. "Markets in Crisis." *Financial Analysts Journal*, vol. 65, no. 1 (January/February):17–24.

"In October 2008, Rodney N. Sullivan, CFA, interviewed John C. Bogle regarding the global financial crisis and his outlook for the future." (Abstract)

Bolton, Patrick, José Scheinkman, and Wei Xiong. 2006. "Executive Compensation and Short-Termist Behaviour in Speculative Markets." *Review of Economic Studies*, vol. 73, no. 3 (July):577–610.

"We present a multiperiod agency model of stock-based executive compensation in a speculative stock market, where investors have heterogeneous beliefs and stock prices may deviate from underlying fundamentals and include a speculative option component. This component arises from the option to sell the stock in the future to potentially overoptimistic investors. We show that optimal compensation contracts may emphasize short-term stock performance, at the expense of long-run fundamental value, as an incentive to induce managers to pursue actions which increase the speculative component in the stock price. Our model provides a different perspective on the recent corporate crisis than the 'rent extraction view' of executive compensation." (p. 577)

Brochet, Francois, Maria Loumioti, and George Serafeim. 2013. "Short-Termism, Investor Clientele, and Corporate Performance." Harvard Business School Accounting & Management Unit Working Paper No. 12-072 (November):1–54 (http://papers.ssrn.com/sol3/papers.cfm?abstract_id=1999484).

"Using conference call transcripts to measure the time horizon that senior executives emphasize when they communicate with investors, we develop a measure of corporate short-termism. We find that the measure of short-termism is associated with various proxies for earnings management, suggesting that our proxy partially captures opportunistic behavior. We also show that firms focusing more on the short-term have a more short-term oriented investor base, and fewer analysts issuing long-term forecasts, suggesting that corporate and capital market short-termism are related. Moreover, consistent with analytical models that emphasize the costly nature of short-termism, we find that short-term oriented firms exhibit lower future accounting and stock market performance and a higher implied cost of capital." (Abstract)

Burton, Edwin T., and Sunit N. Shah. 2013. *Behavioral Finance: Understanding the Social, Cognitive, and Economic Debates*. Hoboken, NJ: John Wiley & Sons.

"Historically, economics has assumed that financial markets are efficient, or that an asset's market price at any given point in time reflects its underlying value. However, there now exists a considerable accumulation of evidence that supports the behavioral finance point of view that this need not be the case. Divided into five comprehensive parts, *Behavioral Finance* offers investors an in-depth guide to the evolving science of behavioral finance. . . . The book explores the Efficient Market Hypothesis, highlights noise trader theory and models including the noted Shleifer model, examines research into psychological behavior pioneered by Daniel Kahneman and Amos Tversky, and offers an examination of serial correlation patterns in stock price data." (Back cover)

Bushee, Brian J. 1998. "The Influence of Institutional Investors on Myopic R&D Investment Behavior." *Accounting Review*, vol. 73, no. 3 (July):305–333.

"This paper examines whether institutional investors create or reduce incentives for corporate managers to reduce investment in research and development (R&D) to meet short-term earnings goals. . . . [The] results indicate that high turnover and momentum trading by institutional investors encourages myopic investment behavior when such institutional investors have extremely high levels of ownership in a firm; otherwise, institutional ownership serves to reduce pressures on managers for myopic investment behavior." (p. 305)

CFA Institute and Edelman. 2013. *Investor Trust Study*: http://www.cfainstitute.org/learning/future/about/Documents/cfa_institute_edelman_investor_trust_study.pdf.

CFA Institute and Edelman surveyed retail and institutional investors in the United States, the United Kingdom, Hong Kong, Canada, and Australia to "better understand the dimensions that shape investor perceptions of trust in investment managers, as well as the actions that help to build trust." (p. 2)

Chesney, Marc, Jacob Stromberg, and Alexander F. Wagner. 2010. "Risk-Taking Incentives, Governance, and Losses in the Financial Crisis." Swiss Finance Institute Research Paper Series No. 10–18 (July):1–48 (http://ideas.repec.org/p/chf/rpseri/rp1018.html).

> "This paper studies the extent to which risk-taking incentives of CEOs and other governance features in a range of years prior to the recent financial crisis were related to the write-downs of U.S. financial institutions during the crisis. We document that institutions whose CEOs had particularly strong risk-taking incentives, weak ownership incentives, and independent boards had the highest write-downs, both in absolute terms and relative to total assets. Furthermore, financial institutions with lower Tier-1 ratios and those with CEOs who earned less than their colleagues at comparable firms had larger write-downs." (Abstract)

Chevalier, Judith, and Glenn Ellison. 1997. "Risk Taking by Mutual Funds as a Response to Incentives." *Journal of Political Economy*, vol. 105, no. 6 (December):1167–1200.

> "This paper examines a potential agency conflict between mutual fund investors and mutual fund companies. Investors would like the fund company to use its judgment to maximize risk-adjusted fund returns. A fund company, however, in its desire to maximize its value as a concern, has an incentive to take actions that increase the inflow of investments. We use a semiparametric model to estimate the shape of the flow-performance relationship for a sample of growth and growth and income funds observed over the 1982–92 period. The shape of the flow-performance relationship creates incentives for fund managers to increase or decrease the riskiness of the fund that are dependent on the fund's year-to-date return. We examine portfolio holdings of mutual funds in September and December and show that mutual funds do alter the riskiness of their portfolios at the end of the year in a manner consistent with these incentives." (p. 1167)

Coase, R.H. 1937. "The Nature of the Firm." *Economica*, vol. 4, no. 16 (November):386–405.

> In Coase's seminal work, he explores the question of why firms exist. He compares the costs of contracting within the firm construct with the costs of using the market pricing mechanism and draws conclusions regarding these costs implied by the fact that firms exist in the marketplace.

Crotty, James. 2009. "Structural Causes of the Global Financial Crisis: A Critical Assessment of the 'New Financial Architecture.'" *Cambridge Journal of Economics*, vol. 33, no. 4 (July):563–580.

> "We are in the midst of the worst financial crisis since the Great Depression. This crisis is the latest phase of the evolution of financial markets under the radical financial deregulation process that began in the late 1970s. This evolution has taken the form of cycles in which deregulation accompanied by rapid financial innovation stimulates powerful financial booms that end in crises. Governments respond to crises with bailouts that allow new expansions to begin. As a result, financial markets have become ever larger and financial crises have become more threatening to society, which forces governments to enact ever larger bailouts. This process culminated in the current global financial crisis, which is so deeply rooted that even unprecedented interventions by affected governments have, thus far, failed to contain it. In this paper we analyse the structural flaws in the financial system that helped bring on the current crisis and discuss prospects for financial reform." (p. 563)

Davidoff, Steven M. 2012. "With Lax Regulation, a Risky Industry Flourishes Offshore." *New York Times Dealbook* (4 September): http://dealbook.nytimes.com/2012/09/04/with-lax-regulation-a-risky-industry-flourishes-offshore/.

> Davidoff examines the entrance of hedge funds into the reinsurance business. He posits that funds are entering the business in response to the fickle desires of investors, who often pull their capital out of funds quickly after poor results. These vehicles provide permanent capital for hedge funds to invest.

De Long, J. Bradford, Andrei Shleifer, Lawrence H. Summers, and Robert J. Waldmann. 1990. "Noise Trader Risk in Financial Markets." *Journal of Political Economy*, vol. 98, no. 4 (August):703–738.

> "We present a simple overlapping generations model of an asset market in which irrational noise traders with erroneous stochastic beliefs both affect prices and earn higher expected returns. The unpredictability of noise traders' beliefs creates a risk in the price of the asset that deters rational arbitrageurs from aggressively betting against them. As a result, prices can diverge significantly from fundamental values even in the absence of fundamental risk. Moreover, bearing a disproportionate amount of risk that they themselves create enables noise traders to earn a higher expected return than rational investors do. The model sheds light on a number of financial anomalies, including the excess volatility of asset prices, the mean reversion of stock returns, the underpricing of closed-end mutual funds, and the Mehra-Prescott equity premium puzzle." (p. 703)

Eisenhardt, Kathleen M. 1989. "Agency Theory: An Assessment and Review." *Academy of Management Review*, vol. 14, no. 1:57–74.

"Agency theory is an important, yet controversial, theory. This paper reviews agency theory, its contributions to organization theory, and the extant empirical work and develops testable propositions. The conclusions are that agency theory (a) offers unique insight into information systems, outcome uncertainty, incentives, and risk and (b) is an empirically valid perspective, particularly when coupled with complementary perspectives. The principal recommendation is to incorporate an agency perspective in studies of the many problems having a cooperative structure." (p. 57)

Epstein, Richard A. 2013. "Grand Theft Treasury." *Defining Ideas* (16 July): http://www.hoover.org/publications/defining-ideas/article/151966.

Epstein examines the role of the government as conservator of Fannie and Freddie. He argues that the government's move to sweep profits from the two firms' shareholders is illegal and explains the rationale behind several lawsuits that have been brought against the government as a result.

Fahlenbrach, Rüdiger, and René M. Stulz. 2011. "Bank CEO Incentives and the Credit Crisis." *Journal of Financial Economics*, vol. 99, no. 1 (January):11–26.

"We investigate whether bank performance during the recent credit crisis is related to chief executive officer (CEO) incentives before the crisis. We find some evidence that banks with CEOs whose incentives were better aligned with the interests of shareholders performed worse and no evidence that they performed better. Banks with higher option compensation and a larger fraction of compensation in cash bonuses for their CEOs did not perform worse during the crisis. Bank CEOs did not reduce their holdings of shares in anticipation of the crisis or during the crisis. Consequently, they suffered extremely large wealth losses in the wake of the crisis." (p. 11)

Frazzini, Andrea, David Kabiller, and Lasse H. Pedersen. 2013. "Buffett's Alpha." Working paper (November):1–45 (http://www.econ.yale.edu/~af227/pdf/Buffett%27s%20Alpha%20-%20Frazzini,%20Kabiller%20and%20Pedersen.pdf).

"Berkshire Hathaway has realized a Sharpe ratio of 0.76, higher than any other stock or mutual fund with a history of more than 30 years, and Berkshire has a significant alpha to traditional risk factors. However, we find that the alpha becomes insignificant when controlling for exposures to Betting-Against Beta and Quality-Minus-Junk factors. Further, we estimate that Buffett's leverage is about 1.6-to-1 on average. Buffett's returns appear to be neither luck nor magic, but, rather, reward for the use of leverage combined with a focus on cheap, safe, quality stocks. Decomposing Berkshires' portfolio into ownership in publicly traded stocks versus wholly-owned private companies, we find that the former performs the best, suggesting that Buffett's returns are more due to stock selection than to his effect on management. These results have broad implications for market efficiency and the implementability of academic factors." (p. 1)

Generation Investment Management. 2012. "Sustainable Capitalism" (15 February): http://www.generationim.com/media/pdf-generation-sustainable-capitalism-v1.pdf.

"The objective of this paper is twofold. First, we make the economic case for mainstreaming Sustainable Capitalism by highlighting the fact that it *does not represent* a trade-off with profit maximization but instead actually fosters superior long-term value creation. Second, we recommend five key actions for immediate adoption that will accelerate the mainstreaming of Sustainable Capitalism by 2020." (p. 1)

Getmansky, Mila, Andrew W. Lo, and Igor Makarov. 2004. "An Econometric Model of Serial Correlation and Illiquidity in Hedge Fund Returns." *Journal of Financial Economics*, vol. 74, no. 3 (December):529–609.

"The returns to hedge funds and other alternative investments are often highly serially correlated. In this paper, we explore several sources of such serial correlation and show that the most likely explanation is illiquidity exposure and smoothed returns. We propose an econometric model of return smoothing and develop estimators for the smoothing profile as well as a smoothing-adjusted Sharpe ratio. For a sample of 908 hedge funds drawn from the TASS database, we show that our estimated smoothing coefficients vary considerably across hedge-fund style categories and may be a useful proxy for quantifying illiquidity exposure." (p. 529)

Goetzmann, William N., Jonathan E. Ingersoll, and Stephen A. Ross. 2003. "High-Water Marks and Hedge Fund Management Contracts." *Journal of Finance*, vol. 58, no. 4 (August):1685–1717.

"Incentive fees for money managers are frequently accompanied by high-water mark provisions that condition the payment of the performance fee upon exceeding the previously achieved maximum share value. In this paper, we show that hedge fund performance fees are valuable to money managers, and conversely, represent a claim on a significant proportion of investor wealth. The high-water mark provisions in these contracts limit the value of the performance fees. We provide a closed-form solution to the cost of the high-water mark contract under certain conditions. Our results provide a framework for valuation of a hedge fund management company." (p. 1685)

Goetzmann, William N., Jonathan Ingersoll, Matthew Spiegel, and Ivo Welch. 2004. "Sharpening Sharpe Ratios." Yale School of Management Working Paper (November):1–44 (http://viking.som.yale.edu/will/hedge/Sharpe.PDF).

> "It is now well known that the Sharpe ratio and other related reward-to-risk measures may be manipulated with option-like strategies. This paper derives the general conditions for achieving the maximum expected Sharpe ratio. Also derived are static rules for achieving the maximum Sharpe ratio with two or more options, as well as a continuum of derivative contracts. The optimal strategy has a truncated right tail and fat left tail. Additionally, the paper provides dynamic rules for increasing the Sharpe ratio.
>
> "In order to address the sensitivity of the Sharpe ratio to informationless, option-like strategies, the paper proposes an alternative measure that is less susceptible to such manipulations. The case for using this alternative ranking metric is particularly compelling in the hedge fund industry where the use of derivatives is unconstrained and manager compensation itself induces a non-linear payoff." (Abstract)

Harris, Milton, and Artur Raviv. 1979. "Optimal Incentive Contracts with Imperfect Information." *Journal of Economic Theory*, vol. 20, no. 2 (April):231–259.

> "It is well known that in situations involving uncertainty, the existence of a complete set of contingent claims is sufficient to assure a Pareto-efficient allocation of resources. . . . The purpose of this paper is to develop a theory of contracts in situations characterized by a divergence of incentives between the two parties and asymmetric information (i.e., moral hazard) with special emphasis on how the possibilities for acquiring information affect the structure of the contract. In particular, we seek to explain the widespread use in areas such as employment and insurance of contracts in which the result of an imperfect (noisy) monitoring process is used to determine the schedule according to which one agent is compensated by another." (p. 231)

Hoshi, Takeo. and Anil K. Kashyap. 2010. "Will the U.S. Bank Recapitalization Succeed? Eight Lessons from Japan." *Journal of Financial Economics*, vol. 97, no. 3 (September):398–417.

> "During the financial crisis that started in 2007, the U.S. government has used a variety of tools to try to rehabilitate the U.S. banking industry. Many of those strategies were also used in Japan to combat its banking problems in the 1990s. There are also a surprising number of other similarities between the current U.S. crisis and the recent Japanese crisis. The Japanese policies were only partially successful in recapitalizing the banks until the economy finally started to recover in 2003. From these unsuccessful attempts, we derive eight lessons.

In light of these eight lessons, we assess the policies the U.S. has pursued. The U.S. has ignored three of the lessons and it is too early to evaluate the U.S. policies with respect to four of the others. So far, the U.S. has avoided Japan's problem of having impaired banks prop up zombie firms." (p. 398)

Ippolito, Richard A. 1992. "Consumer Reaction to Measures of Poor Quality: Evidence from the Mutual Fund Industry." *Journal of Law & Economics*, vol. 35, no. 1 (April):45–70.

"Unless quality is apparent at the point of sale, the market must find ways to ensure the delivery of high-quality products; otherwise, producers have incentives to sell low-quality goods at high-quality prices, thereby assuring a degenerate equilibrium. . . . Despite its prominence in the theoretical literature, direct evidence of consumer response to less-than-promised quality is rarely measured. This market seemingly is ripe for a degenerate equilibrium. There is much noise in performance data across mutual funds and over time, requiring many periods to judge the ability of an investment manager with statistical confidence. . . . I explore the hypothesis that vigilance among mutual fund investors plays an important role in generating an efficient equilibrium in this market. I show that, as long as poor-quality funds exist, an investment algorithm that allocates monies to the latest best performer is rational investor behavior (taking into account transaction costs). This investment algorithm conveys an externality to the market by denying poor-quality funds the opportunity to capture an important market share. I examine empirically whether investors follow these investment rules. I find strong evidence that investors react to new information about product quality in the mutual fund industry, that they react disproportionately where the expected payoffs are higher, and that returns within mutual funds are serially correlated." (pp. 45–47)

Iwatsubo, Kentaro. 2007. "Bank Capital Shocks and Portfolio Risk: Evidence from Japan." *Japan and the World Economy*, vol. 19, no. 2 (March):166–186.

"Despite the downward trend of land prices and the ex post low return on real estate loans, Japanese banks increased their lending to the real estate sector during the 1990s. We argue that this phenomenon can be explained by the risk-shifting incentives of banks and discover that banks with low capital-to-asset ratios and low franchise value chose high-risk assets such as real estate loans. Unlike previous studies, we show that the capital–risk relationship is non-linear and changes from positive to negative as franchise value falls. We also find that a capital adequacy requirement did not prevent risk-taking behavior of under-capitalized banks since they then just issued more subordinated debts to meet this requirement. In contrast, government capital injections led banks to reduce risky loans at the margin. Recapitalization by issuing subordinated debts helped banks recover their capital losses and mitigated the credit crunch, but consequently allowed them to increase their exposure to the real estate sector and worsened the bad loan problems." (p. 166)

Jensen, Michael C., and William H. Meckling. 1976. "Theory of the Firm: Managerial Behavior, Agency Costs, and Ownership Structure." *Journal of Financial Economics*, vol. 3, no. 4 (October):305–360.

"This paper integrates elements from the theory of agency, the theory of property rights, and the theory of finance to develop a theory of the ownership structure of the firm. We define the concept of agency costs, show its relationship to the 'separation and control' issue, investigate the nature of the agency costs generated by the existence of debt and outside equity, demonstrate who bears costs and why, and investigate the Pareto optimality of their existence. We also provide a new definition of the firm and show how our analysis of the factors influencing the creation and issuance of debt and equity claims is a special case of the supply side of the completeness of markets problem." (p. 305)

Kay, John. 2012. "The Kay Review of UK Equity Markets and Long-Term Decision Making: Final Report" (July): http://bis.gov.uk/assets/biscore/business-law/docs/k/12-917-kay-review-of-equity-markets-final-report.pdf.

"In June 2011, the Secretary of State for Business, Innovation and Skills asked [John Kay] to review activity in UK equity markets and its impact on the long-term performance and governance of UK quoted companies. The Review's principal concern has been to ask how well equity markets are achieving their core purposes: to enhance the performance of UK companies and to enable savers to benefit from the activity of these businesses through returns to direct and indirect ownership of shares in UK companies." (p. 9)

Kirkpatrick, Grant. 2009. "The Corporate Governance Lessons from the Financial Crisis." *Financial Market Trends*, vol. 2009, no. 1:1–30 (http://www.oecd.org/finance/financial-markets/42229620.pdf).

"This report analyses the impact of failures and weaknesses in corporate governance on the financial crisis, including risk management systems and executive salaries. It concludes that the financial crisis can be to an important extent attributed to failures and weaknesses in corporate governance arrangements which did not serve their purpose to safeguard against excessive risk taking in a number of financial services companies. Accounting standards and regulatory requirements have also proved insufficient in some areas. Last but not least, remuneration systems have in a number of cases not been closely related to the strategy and risk appetite of the company and its longer term interests. The article also suggests that the importance of qualified board oversight and robust risk management is not limited to financial institutions. The remuneration of boards and senior management also remains a highly controversial issue in many OECD countries. The current turmoil suggests a need for the OECD to re-examine the adequacy of its corporate governance principles in these key areas." (p. 1)

Kotecha, Mahesh, Sharon Ryan, and Roy Weinberger. 2010. "The Future of Structured Finance Ratings after the Financial Crisis." *Journal of Structured Finance*, vol. 15, no. 4 (Winter):67–74.

"The authors believe that the rating agency reforms underway in Europe and the United States, as well as at the agencies themselves, are steps in the right direction but do not go far enough to ensure accuracy and timeliness of ratings. Most importantly, they fail to address the conflict-ridden rating agency compensation system. The authors believe that credibility of ratings cannot be restored until rating agencies are paid not by the sell side or the buy side, but by both the buy side and the sell side, via a transaction charge on new issues and secondary market trades. Their proposal is to pay for ratings via an industry fund such as has been operated for over two decades by the U.S. Municipal Securities Rulemaking Board (MSRB), albeit on a smaller scale and for a more limited purpose, for the benefit of the municipal securities markets. Carefully structured, such a compensation system would give rating agencies more appropriate incentives to produce more accurate and timely ratings that can hold up through both up and down markets." (Summary: http://www.iijournals.com/doi/abs/10.3905/JSF.2010.15.4.067#sthash.iLpdBp3N.dpbs)

Labaton Sucharow. 2013. "Wall Street in Crisis: A Perfect Storm Looming." U.S. Financial Services Industry Survey (July): http://www.secwhistlebloweradvocate.com/.

The law firm of Labaton Sucharow conducted a survey on the state of ethics on Wall Street and found some alarming and troubling results.

Laffont, Jean-Jacques, and David Martimort. 2002. *The Theory of Incentives: The Principal-Agent Model*. Princeton, NJ: Princeton University Press.

"This book focuses on the principal-agent model, the 'simple' situation where a principal, or company, delegates a task to a single agent through a contract—the essence of management and contract theory. How does the owner or manager of a firm align the objectives of its various members to maximize profits? Following a brief historical overview showing how the problem of incentives has come to the fore in the past two centuries, the authors devote the bulk of their work to exploring principal-agent models and various extensions thereof in light of three types of information problems: adverse selection, moral hazard, and non-verifiability. Offering an unprecedented look at a subject vital to industrial organization, labor economics, and behavioral economics, this book is set to become the definitive resource for students, researchers, and others who might find themselves pondering what contracts, and the incentives they embody, are really all about." (Summary: http://www.amazon.com/books/dp/0691091846)

Lambert, Richard A. and David F Larcker. 2004. "Stock Options, Restricted Stock, and Incentives." Working paper, University of Pennsylvania (April):1–46 (http://papers.ssrn.com/sol3/papers.cfm?abstract_id=527822).

"Prior work has suggested that options represent an inefficient form of compensation because the value placed on an option by a risk-averse employee is much less than the cost of the option from the perspective of the firm. However, much of this work fails to properly incorporate the incentive effect of option-based contracts into their analysis. We use agency theory to model the optimal mix of options and stock in the compensation contract. In contrast to prior work, we show that restricted stock is generally not the optimal contract form, and that option-based contracts have both efficiency and incentive advantages." (p. 2)

Lan, Yingcong, Neng Wang, and Jinqiang Yang. 2013. "The Economics of Hedge Funds." *Journal of Financial Economics*, vol. 110, no. 2 (November):300–323.

"Hedge fund managers trade off the benefits of leveraging on the alpha-generating strategy against the costs of inefficient fund liquidation. In contrast to the standard risk-seeking intuition, even with a constant-return-to-scale alpha-generating strategy, a risk-neutral manager becomes endogenously risk-averse and decreases leverage following poor performance to increase the fund's survival likelihood. Our calibration suggests that management fees are the majority of the total compensation. Money flows, managerial restart options, and management ownership increase the importance of high-water-mark-based incentive fees, but management fees remain the majority. Investors' valuation[s] of fees are highly sensitive to their assessments of the manager's skill." (p. 300)

Laverty, Kevin J. 1996. "Economic 'Short-Termism': The Debate, the Unresolved Issues, and the Implications for Management Practice and Research." *Academy of Management Review*, vol. 21, no. 3 (July):825–860.

"In many crucial decisions, the course of action that is most desirable over the long run is not the best course of action in the short term. This is the dilemma addressed by the ongoing debate over economic 'short-termism,' sparked by contentions that U.S. firms are losing to overseas competitors because U.S. management is unwilling or unable to invest in the long run. I argue that the debate has suffered from a limited focus; to address this problem, I present a framework that addresses organizational and individual as well as economic perspectives. I offer a review of concepts, analysis, and evidence, and I suggest a cross-discipline, multilevel research agenda for advancing understanding of this vital topic." (p. 825)

Lim, Jongha, Berk A. Sensoy, and Michael S. Weisbach. 2013. "Indirect Incentives of Hedge Fund Managers." NBER Working Paper No. 18903 (March):1–45.

"Indirect incentives exist in the money management industry when good current performance increases future inflows of new capital, leading to higher future fees. We quantify the magnitude of indirect performance incentives for hedge fund managers. Flows respond quickly and strongly to performance; lagged performance has a monotonically decreasing impact on flows as lags increase up to two years. Conservative estimates indicate that indirect incentives for the average fund are four times as large as direct incentives from incentive fees and returns to managers' own investment in the fund. For new funds, indirect incentives are seven times as large as direct incentives. Combining direct and indirect incentives, for each dollar generated for their investors in a given year, managers receive close to another dollar in direct performance fees plus the present value of future fees over the expected life of the fund. Older and capacity constrained funds have considerably weaker relations between future flows and performance, leading to weaker indirect incentives. There is no evidence that direct contractual incentives are stronger when market-based indirect incentives are weaker." (Abstract)

Lo, Andrew W. 2002. "The Statistics of Sharpe Ratios." *Financial Analysts Journal*, vol. 58, no. 4 (July/August):36–52.

"The building blocks of the Sharpe ratio—expected returns and volatilities—are unknown quantities that must be estimated statistically and are, therefore, subject to estimation error. This raises the natural question: How accurately are Sharpe ratios measured? To address this question, I derive explicit expressions for the statistical distribution of the Sharpe ratio using standard asymptotic theory under several sets of assumptions for the return-generating process—independently and identically distributed returns, stationary returns, and with time aggregation. I show that monthly Sharpe ratios cannot be annualized by multiplying by $\sqrt{12}$ except under very special circumstances, and I derive the correct method of conversion in the general case of stationary returns. In an illustrative empirical example of mutual funds and hedge funds, I find that the annual Sharpe ratio for a hedge fund can be overstated by as much as 65 percent because of the presence of serial correlation in monthly returns, and once this serial correlation is properly taken into account, the rankings of hedge funds based on Sharpe ratios can change dramatically." (p. 36)

Lynch, Anthony W., and David K. Musto. 2003. "How Investors Interpret Past Fund Returns." *Journal of Finance*, vol. 58, no. 5 (October):2033–2058.

"The literature documents a convex relation between past returns and fund flows of mutual funds. We show this to be consistent with fund incentives, because funds discard exactly those strategies which underperform. Past returns tell less about the future performance of funds which discard, so flows are less sensitive to them when they are poor. Our model predicts that strategy changes only occur after bad performance, and that bad performers who change strategy have dollar flow and future performance that are less sensitive to current performance than those that do not. Empirical tests support both predictions." (p. 2033)

Mas-Colell, Andreu, Michael D. Whinston, and Jerry R. Green. 1995. *Microeconomic Theory*. New York: Oxford University Press.

"The authors set out to create a solid organizational foundation upon which to build the effective teaching tool for microeconomic theory. The result presents unprecedented depth of coverage in all the essential topics, while allowing professors to 'tailor-make' their course to suit personal priorities and style. Topics such as noncooperative game theory, information economics, mechanism design, and general equilibrium under uncertainty receive the attention that reflects their stature within the discipline. The authors devote an entire section to game theory alone, making it 'free-standing' to allow instructors to return to it throughout the course when convenient. Discussion is clear, accessible, and engaging, enabling the student to gradually acquire confidence as well as proficiency. Extensive exercises within each chapter help students to hone their skills, while the text's appendix of terms, fully cross-referenced throughout the previous five sections, offers an accessible guide to the subject matter's terminology. Teachers of microeconomics need no longer rely upon scattered lecture notes to supplement their textbooks. Deftly written by three of the field's most influential scholars, *Microeconomic Theory* brings the readability, comprehensiveness, and versatility to the first-year graduate classroom that has long been missing." (Online Summary)

Meulbroek, Lisa K., and Mark L. Mitchell. J. Harold Mulherin, Jeffry M. Netter, and Annette B. Poulsen. 1990. "Shark Repellents and Managerial Myopia: An Empirical Test." *Journal of Political Economy*, vol. 98, no. 5, part 1 (October):1108–1117.

"While the evidence supporting takeover-induced shortsightedness is largely anecdotal, a recent paper by Stein (1988) develops a formal model in which the threat of takeovers encourages myopic behavior on the part of managers. A central prediction of Stein's model is that firms that construct barriers to takeover are able to increase profitable long-term investments such as research and development (R & D). This paper provides empirical evidence that firms actually decrease R & D intensity after the introduction of shark repellents, thus failing to support Stein's prediction. The findings suggest that takeover impediments may reduce incentives to engage in long-term investments." (pp. 1108–1109)

Mider, Zachary R. 2013. "A Hedge Fund Tax Dodge Uses Bermuda Reinsurers." *Bloomberg Businessweek* (21 February): http://www.businessweek.com/printer/articles/98250-a-hedge-fund-tax-dodge-uses-bermuda-reinsurers.

Mider discusses the reinsurance company set up by the hedge fund Paulson. He describes the vehicle as a method for hedge fund manager John Paulson and others to avoid paying taxes. He also briefly discusses other hedge funds that set up similar vehicles.

Miller, Gary J. 2008. "Solutions to Principal–Agent Problems in Firms." In *Handbook of New Institutional Economics*. Edited by Claude Ménard and Mary M. Shirley. Berlin: Springer-Verlag:349–370.

Miller reflects on Coase's idea that the costs of the price mechanism drive the existence of firms. He explores several solutions to the principal–agent problem in various contexts within the firm and concludes that there is no catch-all solution. Instead, the solution varies depending on the characteristics of the firm that give rise to the specific instance of the problem.

Poole, William. 2009. "Moral Hazard: The Long-Lasting Legacy of Bailouts." *Financial Analysts Journal*, vol. 65, no. 6 (November/December):17–23.

"The U.S. government appears to be committed to supporting any large bank that gets into trouble. A bailout environment distorts risk assessments. Debt capital flows more readily to large institutions, even inefficient ones, than to small ones. This article proposes reforms to the U.S. financial system. A change in incentives is needed. Phasing out the deductibility of interest on all business tax returns would reduce the incentive for leverage. Another reform would require all banks to issue 10-year subordinated notes, which would provide a large capital cushion. Banks would have to go to market every year to replace maturing subordinated debt, which would greatly enhance market discipline." (Abstract)

Poole, William. 2010. "Ending Moral Hazard." *Financial Analysts Journal*, vol. 66, no. 3 (May/June):17–24.

"FAJ editor Rodney Sullivan, CFA, recently sat down with former Federal Reserve Bank president William Poole for an interview about the fallout from the global market crisis and how to end the moral hazard arising from government bailouts." (Abstract)

Rappaport, Alfred. 2005. "The Economics of Short-Term Performance Obsession." *Financial Analysts Journal*, vol. 61, no. 3 (May/June):65–79.

"In theory, discounted cash flows (DCFs) set prices in well-functioning capital markets. In practice, investment managers attach substantial weight in stock selection to short-term performance, particularly earnings and tracking error. Corporate executives blame this behavior for their own obsession with short-term earnings. Are stock prices likely to allocate financial resources efficiently when short-term earnings dominate investment decisions? Can investment managers who identify stocks as mispriced on a DCF basis earn excess returns? This article explains why maximizing long-term cash flow is the most effective way to create value for shareholders and charts a course for alleviating the obsession with short-term performance." (Abstract)

Rappaport, Alfred. 2011. *Saving Capitalism from Short-Termism: How to Build Long-Term Value and Take Back Our Financial Future*. New York: McGraw-Hill.

"[Rappaport] delivers a clarion call for conquering this addiction to short-term profit and getting on the path to building long-term value. His solution to short-termism is simple but profound: Business leaders must align the interests of corporate and investment managers with those of their shareholders and beneficiaries. Part 1 of the book examines short-termism in publicly traded companies and the investment management community. Part 2 presents an action plan for raising profit horizons by aligning the interests of corporate and investment managers with those of their shareholders and beneficiaries." (Press Release Summary)

Ross, Stephen A. 1973. "The Economic Theory of Agency: The Principal's Problem." *American Economic Review*, vol. 63, no. 2 (May):134–139.

Ross explores the principal–agent problem and defines classes of utility functions and payoff structures that give rise to Pareto-optimal outcomes.

Schumpeter, Joseph. 1954. *History of Economic Analysis*. New York: Oxford University Press.

"At the time of his death in 1950, Joseph Schumpeter—one of the great economists of the first half of the 20th century—was working on his monumental *History of Economic Analysis*. A complete history of efforts to understand the subject of economics from ancient Greece to the present, this book is an important contribution to the history of ideas as well as to economics. Although never fully completed, it has gained recognition as a modern classic due to its broad scope and original examination of significant historical events. . . . Major topics include the techniques of economic analysis, contemporaneous developments in other sciences, and the sociology of economics; economic writings from Plato and Aristotle up through the time of Adam Smith, including the medieval scholastics and natural-law philosophers; the work of Malthus, Mill, Ricardo, Marx, and the important European economists; the history, sociology, psychology, and economics of the period 1879–1914; and modern economic developments. Schumpeter perceived economics as a human science, and this lucid and insightful volume reflects that perception, creating a work that is of major importance to the history of economics." (Online Summary)

Shleifer, Andrei, and Robert W. Vishny. 1990. "Equilibrium Short Horizons of Investors and Firms." *American Economic Review*, vol. 80, no. 2 (May):148–153.

"This paper attempts to explain the often lamented pursuit by investors of short-term capital gains and the selection by firms of short-term investment projects. Our starting point is the observation that, in practice, arbitrage (trading based on knowledge that the price of an asset is different from its fundamental value) is cheaper for assets that cannot stay mispriced for long (short-term assets) than for assets that can (long-term assets). (p. 148)

"Arbitrage generally serves the useful social function of bringing asset prices closer to fundamental values. Arbitrage itself, however, is guided by maximization of arbitrage profits. We [show] that the private costs and benefits of arbitrage lead to its clustering on the trading of short-term assets. This clustering in turn leads to systematically more accurate pricing of short-term assets than of long-term assets, even though efficient capital allocation and managerial evaluation might be better served by the opposite bias." (p. 153)

Sirri, Erik R., and Peter Tufano. 1998. "Costly Search and Mutual Fund Flows." *Journal of Finance*, vol. 53, no. 5 (October):1589–1622.

"This paper studies the flows of funds into and out of equity mutual funds. Consumers base their fund purchase decisions on prior performance information, but do so asymmetrically, investing disproportionately more in funds that performed very well the prior period. Search costs seem to be an important determinant of fund flows. High performance appears to be most salient for funds that exert higher marketing effort, as measured by higher fees. Flows are directly related to the size of the fund's complex as well as the current media attention received by the fund, which lower consumers' search costs." (p. 1589)

Smith, Alison, and Stephen Foley. 2013. "Criticism of Short-Term Investing Grows after Woodford Departure." *Financial Times* (18 October): http://www.ft.com/cms/s/0/34a2abba-37e7-11e3-8668-00144feab7de.html#axzz2qtdHBQFB.

Smith and Foley springboard from Neil Woodford's decision to leave Invesco Perpetual to a general discussion of investor short-termism in UK markets.

Sorkin, Andrew Ross. 2013. "On Wall Street, a Culture of Greed Won't Let Go." *New York Times* (16 July):B1.

Sorkin discusses a survey produced by Labaton Sucharow on the state of ethics on Wall Street. The survey's results show that employees at banks do not believe that their colleagues act ethically and often do not believe that they themselves act ethically either.

Spence, Michael, and Richard Zeckhauser. 1971. "Insurance, Information, and Individual Action." *American Economic Review*, vol. 61, no. 2 (May):380–387.

"This paper looks at some intricacies and difficulties that arise in the real world operation of contingent claims markets. Insurance contracts, the most readily observable and perhaps most important example of contingent claims markets in action, provide the focus for our discussion." (p. 380)

The authors find that in cases in which the insurer can monitor the insured, no adverse incentive problem occurs. When monitoring is impossible or incomplete, however, appropriate incentives for action by the insured will not be achieved.

St. Anthony, Neal. 2013. "St. Anthony: Pine River Takes on Housing Bust as Investor and Landlord." *Star Tribune* (26 May): http://www.startribune.com/business/208912211.html.

St. Anthony discusses Pine River's publicly traded firms: Two Harbors, a real estate investment trust, and Silver Bay, which specializes in buying distressed property. He goes through the evolution of these firms and discusses why Pine River thought they were good investments to make given current market conditions.

Stein, Jeremy. 1988. "Takeover Threats and Managerial Myopia." *Journal of Political Economy*, vol. 96, no. 1 (February):61–80.

"This paper examines the familiar argument that takeover pressure can be damaging because it leads managers to sacrifice long-term interests in order to boost current profits. If stockholders are imperfectly informed, temporarily low earnings may cause the stock to become undervalued, increasing the likelihood of a takeover at an unfavorable price; hence the managerial concern with current bottom line. The magnitude of the problem depends on a variety of factors, including the attitudes and beliefs of shareholders, the extent to which corporate raiders have inside information, and the degree to which managers are concerned with retaining control of their firms." (p. 61)

Stein, Jeremy. 1989. "Efficient Capital Markets, Inefficient Firms: A Model of Myopic Corporate Behavior." *Quarterly Journal of Economics*, vol. 104, no. 4 (November):655–669.

"This paper develops a model of inefficient managerial behavior in the face of a rational stock market. In an effort to mislead the market about their firms' worth, managers forsake good investments so as to boost current earnings. In equilibrium the market is efficient and is not fooled: It correctly conjectures that there will be earnings inflation, and adjusts for this in making inferences. Nonetheless, managers, who take the market's conjectures as fixed, continue to behave myopically. The model is useful in assessing evidence that has been presented in the 'myopia' debate. It also yields some novel implications regarding firm structure and the limits of [integration]." (p. 655)

Sullivan, Rodney N. 2009. "Governance: Travel and Destinations." *Financial Analysts Journal*, vol. 65, no. 4 (July/August):6–10.

"A global crisis of confidence should never be driven by poor vigilance over governance. Sadly, however, that is our story. A serious breakdown in trust between society at large and capital market agents is upon us. Out of the morass, however, arises an opportunity for our profession to deal effectively with the challenge. Now is our moment to demonstrate true governance leadership—something so important that it should be hard to think about anything else. To seize this moment requires that we go beyond the well-worn crisis travelogue and suggest an itinerary that will bring us to a sustainable governance destination." (p. 6)

Timiraos, Nick, and Alan Zibel. 2013. "Easing of Mortgage Curb Weighed." *Wall Street Journal* (24 July):C1.

Timiraos and Zibel discuss proposed changes to the laws that require banks to keep a portion of the mortgage securities they sell to investors. The authors discuss the pros and cons of changing the requirements for qualified residential mortgages and explain which entities are in favor of such changes.

Wilson, Robert. 1968. "On the Theory of Syndicates." *Econometrica*, vol. 36, no. 1 (January):119–132.

"A syndicate is defined to be a group of individuals who must make a common decision under uncertainty that will result in a payoff to be shared jointly among them. In this paper, the normative criterion of Pareto optimality is employed to determine the construction, and conditions for existence, of a group utility function and a consensus of the members' probability assessments." (p. 119)

Zhou, Chen. 2009. "Are Banks Too Big to Fail? Measuring Systemic Importance of Financial Institutions." Working paper (1 December):1–40 (http://ssrn.com/abstract=1546384).

"We consider three measures on the systemic importance of a financial institution within a[n] interconnected financial system. Based on the measures, we study the relation between the size of a financial institution and its systemic importance. From both theoretical model and empirical analysis, we find that in analyzing the systemic risk posed by one financial institution to the system, size should not be considered as a proxy of systemic importance. In other words, the 'too big to fail' argument is not always valid, and alternative measures on systemic importance should be considered. We provide the estimation methodology of systemic importance measures under the multivariate Extreme Value Theory (EVT) framework." (p. 1)

Made in the USA
Monee, IL
24 June 2026

55647560R00036